Vocabulary Myths

Applying Second Language Research

to Classroom Teaching

Keith S. Folse, Ph.D.

University of Central Florida

Ann Arbor
The University of Michigan Press

Published in the United States of America by
The University of Michigan Press
Typeset by Sans Serif Inc.
Manufactured in the United States of America
Printed on acid-free paper

2011   2010   2009   2008   6   5   4   3

Library of Congress Cataloging-in-Publication Data

Folse, Keith S.
   Vocabulary myths : applying second language research to classroom teaching / Keith S. Folse.
     p.m.
  ISBN 0-472-03029-9 (pbk.)
   1. English language—Study and teaching—Foreign speakers. 2. Vocabulary—Study and teaching. I. Title.

  PE1128.A2F575 2004
  428.1'071—dc22   2004046034

ISBN 978-0-472-03029-3 (pbk.)

Dedication

This book, which describes the learning of vocabulary in languages as diverse as English, Japanese, Spanish, and Arabic, is dedicated to my first foreign language teacher. I can still remember the magic of the first day of class when Mrs. de Montluzin came into the room and said, "I'm going to tell you something in French today, and I'll tell you the same thing nine months from now to see how much French you have learned. *Je m'appelle Madame de Montluzin et je suis votre professeur de français. Je vais vous enseigner le français. J'espère que vous aimez ce cours de français.*"

With these French words, vocabulary that I did not know, my curiosity in foreign languages was piqued. I can honestly say that I would most likely not be a language teacher today if I had not had the opportunity to be a student in her class. Therefore, it is with extreme pride that I dedicate this book to Mrs. Emily de Montluzin, who taught me two years of French in a small high school in Mississippi and thereby started me in this great field of language study.

KSF

Preface

For years, second language learners have complained about their lack of vocabulary in their new language. During this time, experts in our field did not give much importance to vocabulary, as evidenced in the dearth of second language research studies on vocabulary. Instead, second language research dealt with syntax, motivation, contrastive analysis, or learning styles. However, since the mid-1990s there has been a mini-explosion of research on second language vocabulary issues such as student needs, teaching techniques, learner strategies, and incidental learning. Finally, we are arriving at some answers to key questions that both teachers and students have had about vocabulary for many years.

We know that vocabulary **is** important. One of the myths that I have heard over and over in my many years of teaching is that vocabulary is not a big deal. At numerous conference presentations and in numerous journal articles (and even in classes that I have observed), we were told that all you had to do was provide comprehensible input and as a result, the new language would somehow magically fall into place. Students were told to read for "gist," to listen for the overall idea, and not to worry about "the details" too much. The problem was that the students themselves recognized that they could not really understand a large number of the words in the reading or listening passage and, hence, the meaning of the actual passage. Comprehensible input was therefore neither **comprehensible** nor **input**. The students recognized the true value of vocabulary in second language learning, something that our profession is finally beginning to address.

Teachers were told that vocabulary was not a big deal. We were told not to teach words in isolation and instead were told that context was key, which is another of the myths about second language vocabulary. No one is denying that context is important in real communication, but if the learner does not know a large number of words, then there is no context to use for clues. Context clues in the real world are of limited value, especially if the learner does not know enough of the words in the clues themselves. Using context clues to figure out new vocabulary is a good coping skill; however, it is not a very efficient way *for second language learners* to learn a lot of vocabulary. This myth that promotes using context clues over learning lots of vocabulary is based on the overzealous comparisons of learning a first language and a second language.

One source of the lack of attention to vocabulary is that our field tends to be dominated by teachers and curriculum planners whose primary experience with a foreign language has been with English, French, German, or another language that is similar to English in many ways. In learning a second language, the learners' needs in terms of grammar, pronunciation, writing, and vocabulary will vary according to the first language. What I am talking about here goes far beyond simple contrastive analysis.

In terms of vocabulary, which is the scope of this book, different native languages present different issues when learning a second language. My initial second language study was of French and then Spanish. Later, I studied Arabic, Malay, German, and then Japanese. Though the actual memorization and other aspects of learning these languages were similar, learning vocabulary in French and Spanish was a very different experience from learning vocabulary in Malay but even more so in Arabic and Japanese.

As an English speaker learning French and Spanish, I found many cognates. For example, just about any English noun that ends in -*tion* will be the same word in Spanish but with -*ción*. Thus, without ever being exposed to the words in Spanish, I can predict that *edición*, *construcción*, and *manifestación* are actual Spanish words. In Japanese, however, even after six years of being a principal at a school and interacting in Japanese with students, teachers, and parents all day, I have no idea how to say these words in Japanese. To be sure, there are English cognates in Japanese, Malay, and Arabic, but their extent in these languages is far less than it is in Romance languages (or German).

As I studied Arabic, I learned not to translate the word *be* because in the present tense it does not exist. In Japanese, I learned to say "Tadaima" when I arrived home and "Itadakimasu" before I ate anything, but these words do not have a literal translation in English. In Malay, I learned to use different words for different types of bananas, and I learned to divide the day into *pagi, tengahari, petang,* and *malam* although these new words (and concepts even) did not really match up with the division of our English day into *morning, afternoon, evening,* and *night*. In sum, I had the opportunity to see that learning vocabulary in a second language sometimes presented new and different problems for L2 (second language) learners in addition to the normal problem of learning a lot of new information.

Why my interest in vocabulary? My interest in vocabulary started quite early. I was lucky enough to grow up in south Louisiana, an area where *beaucoup,* pronounced as boo-koo, was as much a part of my everyday English vocabulary as *neutral ground* (in general English: the medium between two sides of a street) or *etoufee* (in general English: a thick stew with seafood or meat). I learned early on that we talked funny, and a lot of this was due to our words.

My early exposure to foreign languages was limited to Spanish and French, and I was always fascinated by the way they sounded and why they sounded like that. If I woke up early enough, I could listen to some Cajun French on the handful of television channels that broadcast programs in Cajun French at dawn. However, a huge source of my interest in foreign languages was through another TV program, "I Love Lucy." Lucy jokingly added an *-o* to English words, and suddenly she was speaking Spanish—albeit broken Spanish, but I did not know for many years that she was just joking.

In high school, my first foreign language experience was with Mrs. Emily de Montluzin, who really opened up my eyes to foreign languages. Each week we had a French vocabulary test. Vocabulary was emphasized through explicit teaching, and vocabulary was tested, and I learned not only the importance of vocabulary but also French vocabulary. Armed with words and good language skills, I was able to use this knowledge to improve my French. I used this same strategy with Spanish, then Arabic, Malay, German, and Japanese.

In teaching students in and from countries all over the world, I have seen them struggle and—for the most part—succeed in their learning process. Although the outside of the classroom was different—from tropical jungles in Malaysia to snow-covered mountains in Japan, to the desert in Saudi Arabia—students appreciate good instruction in vocabulary, which includes teaching words that students need to know, giving many good examples of the words, and holding students accountable for the words through appropriate practice activities and systematic testing. It is hoped that the material presented in this book will enable you to have a better understanding of how vocabulary works for L2 learners, L2 teachers, L2 curriculum designers, and materials writers.

Book Organization

The organization of this book is quite simple. An introduction section offers a brief summary of some basic concepts in second language vocabulary. The bulk of the book revolves around chapters representing each of the eight myths discussed. These myths are not presented in any special order, and their relevant discussions are not mutually exclusive. Because of this, you may see a study explained in depth for one myth, discussed briefly in another myth, and enumerated on a summary table of research in another. Each chapter begins with a section called **In the Real World** that describes an actual teaching situation. This is followed by a section called **What the Research Says**. Finally, each chapter ends with a list of pedagogical applications called **What You Can Do**. The book closes with a brief conclusion to the discussion.

The sole aim of this book is to connect in a straightforward way the growing body of second language vocabulary research with teacher actions in classrooms. As you read this book, see how many of the examples and descriptions in each of the myths you can relate to as either teacher or student. I sincerely hope that this research and the discussions will have an impact on the way you view the learning and teaching of vocabulary in a second language.

Keith S. Folse
Orlando, Florida
January 2004

Acknowledgments

This book is the result of years of teaching and studying languages in many settings all over the world. I thank the teachers and students that I have been fortunate enough to work with.

I wish to thank Batia Laufer and Jan Hulstijn for their encouragement and help during my early studies of second language vocabulary. Their works were some of the first vocabulary research that I read, and I was attracted immediately to the great designs of their research as well as the practicality of their research questions.

Finally, I am especially grateful to Kelly Sippell, senior ESL acquisitions editor at the University of Michigan Press, for her constant encouragement and hard work in helping to make our preliminary idea become the book that *Vocabulary Myths* has become.

Contents

An Introduction to
Second Language Vocabulary

THE PURPOSE OF THIS BOOK is to discuss eight pervasive myths or misconceptions regarding the teaching and learning of second language vocabulary. To better appreciate this discussion, a simple overview of basic concepts in second language vocabulary study are in order.

This overview is divided into two parts. The first part addresses the question of what we mean by the term *vocabulary* when nonnative speakers are studying a target language. Here we look at single words, set phrases, variable phrases, phrasal verbs, and idioms. The second part covers seven components of what it means to know a word. While the definition of the word is an obvious component, others include a word's frequency, register, spelling, and collocations. This last component in particular is important for learners to be able to use a word correctly.

Before you read any further, how would you answer these questions:

1. **What are the different kinds of vocabulary in English?**
2. **What are the components of knowing a word? Or, what does it mean to know a word?**

PART I: What Is "a Vocabulary"?

When we talk about learning vocabulary in another language, we immediately envision a list of words. Upon more careful inspection of our imaginary list, we would probably see that, for the most part, our list is composed of single unit words such as *dozen, awkward,* and *feedback.* However, vocabulary (or "vocabularies," as our students mistakenly call it when they assume that *vocabulary* is a count noun, as in "Teacher, I learned 10 vocabularies last night.") can be much more than just a single unit word.

There are in fact many different kinds of vocabulary items or "words." This is especially true when nonnative learners eye their target language as linguistic outsiders. One simple way to look at vocabulary for second language learners is **single words, set phrases, variable phrases, phrasal verbs,** and **idioms**.

Single Words

This is the group that most people think of first. By far, this group includes the bulk of the vocabulary of any language. This group includes not only more items but also more frequently used items:

- animals: *cat, dog, elephant*
- time periods: *Monday, January, today*
- countries: *Egypt, Mexico, Somalia*
- actions in the past: *flew, stayed, went*
- descriptions: *happy, amazing, destructive*
- counters: *dozen, plenty, decade*

Despite the name, however, this group also includes multiword vocabulary. Consider the words *thunderstorm* and *ice storm.* Both are single "words" even though *ice storm* requires two words to express its concept while *thunderstorm* requires only one. The number of actual words in the vocabulary item is the result of spelling conventions peculiar to English, not a vocabulary-related issue. The explanation of whether a compound vocabulary item is written as one word or two does not appear to be semantically based. For example, a cloth for a table is a *tablecloth* (one word) while a cup for coffee is a *coffee cup* (two words). Other examples of compound nouns being written as one word or two words on the apparent whims of English spelling conventions include *graveyard, homework,* and *holiday* versus *traffic light, bread box,* and *table scraps.*

Set Phrases

These phrases consist of more than one word and do not usually change. For example, in the set phrase *in other words,* we cannot say *with other words* or *in other terms* or *in other remarks* or *in other phrases* or other variations, even though *terms* and *remarks* and perhaps *phrases* might seem to be able to fit.

- *in other words*   not: *in other terms* (but *terms* are words)
- *raining cats and dogs*   not: *raining kittens and puppies* (you can only have the adult animals)
- *the bottom line*   not: *the lowest line* (but the *bottom* is the *lowest*)
- *all of a sudden*   not: *most of a sudden* (it's either all or nothing— but we don't have *none of a sudden* either)
- *it's up to you*   not: *it's above to you* (but *up* and *above* are close synonyms)

Other set phrases must be worded in a certain order even though rearranging the ordering would not really affect the meaning. However, English conventions have locked these phrases into only one possible ordering:

- *raining cats and dogs*   not: *raining dogs and cats*
- *up and down*   not: *down and up*

- *from head to toe* not: *from toe to head*
- *back and forth* not: *forth and back*
- *to and fro* not: *fro and to*
- *ladies and gentlemen* not: *gentlemen and ladies*
  (though common in
  many languages)

Variable Phrases

While most of the components in variable phrases will stay the same, there is some variation. The variation often involves personal pronouns or some sort of possessive. For example, a usual form of the opening line of many business letters, especially from companies writing to inform you of a problem, is It *has come to our attention that* . . . . This line could easily be It *has come to my attention that* . . . if it were coming from your boss or coworker.

How would you complete these sentences?

Situation A: You studied French in high school for one year, then you studied two years in college (with a one-year interval between the two years), and then you studied a month or two here and there. A friend asks you, "How long have you been studying French?" You answer, "Well, let me see. I guess I've been studying French _____ for about eight years." What phrase would you use to complete this sentence with the idea that sometimes you did this and sometimes you did not?

Situation B: It's 6:00 P.M. When you woke up this morning, it was raining. It stopped mid-morning. Just before noon, it started raining again but only briefly. Later, it rained from 2:00 P.M. to 3:30 P.M. About an hour ago, it started drizzling again. If you were to call someone in a different part of the country and that person asked you about the weather where you are, you might say, "Well, it's been raining _____ all day long." What phrase would you use to indicate the nature of today's rain?

The answer to both Situations A and B is *off and on* or *on and off*. (I personally never say *on and off* and was quite surprised to hear others say this. I wonder if this is regional usage.)

Another example of a variable phrase is *It has come to _____ attention that* + S + V. You know that this phrase is formal and serious. You also know that it is used more in writing than in speaking. You know that if you receive a letter that begins *It has come to our attention that you . . . ,* the message is usually not good. This phrase really means something like "I'm going to tell you what you did and the problem that it has caused." This phrase is not about knowing *it* + *has come* + *to* + (anyone's attention). This is a good example of where a learner needs to know this whole phrase as a single phrase or single vocabulary item. The only thing that could change in this expression is the possessive adjective before the word *attention,* with *my* and *our* being much more common than *her* or *their* although, in theory, any possessive adjective could work here.

Phrasal Verbs

Your awareness of phrasal verbs is critical to your ability as a native speaker to provide comprehensible input for your ESL students. Native speakers have no idea that they are using phrasal verbs, nor do they see why these words are so hard for ESL students to deal with.

What is a **phrasal verb?** A phrasal verb consists of two or three words. The first word is always a verb. The second word in a phrasal verb is a preposition or particle/adverb. If there is a third word, it is usually a preposition. A good example is *put up with,* meaning to tolerate or stand.

. Many verbs can serve as the verb in a phrasal verb, but common ones include *put, take, come, call, make, go,* and *get.*

> **examples:** *put away, put off, put on, put up, put up with, put down, come back, come off as, come up with, come down with*

Understanding phrasal verbs is problematic for ESL students for four reasons. First, phrasal verbs are extremely common in English. (They occur in Germanic languages but not in Romance languages.) You cannot function in English without knowing a large number of phrasal verbs very well. Therefore, ESL learners must know the meanings of the more frequent ones even in the simplest of exchanges. In trying to provide good comprehensible input for students, ESL teachers must be aware of phrasal verbs so they can better gauge the level of their input. What appears comprehensible may not be so, and the biggest factor may be phrasal verbs.

A second problem is that phrasal verbs are rarely transparent in meaning. Knowing the parts of the phrasal verb does not equal knowing the whole phrasal verb. The example that I always use in teacher training workshops to get people's attention is *throw up*. If you know *throw* (as many of our low-level students do) and if you know *up* (as almost any beginner does), it should follow then—but does not—that you will know the meaning of *throw up*.

Consider these examples that have *call* as a base. Each phrasal verb has a very different meaning.

1. He **called off** the meeting.
2. I **called up** Joe to invite him to the game.
3. Can you **call** me **back** later?
4. The teacher **called on** the sleeping student.
5. Mr. Graves **called** me **in** to discuss my job performance.
6. She **called out** the answers.

In addition, there is another level of meaning that phrasal verbs can express in English, and this subtle sociolinguistic meaning is very hard for our ESL students to capture. Phrasal verbs are one way that we express informality in English conversation. Unlike English, many languages have syntactic ways of expressing informality and familiarity—for example, verb endings vary depending on whether the subject is the formal or informal *you*. Consider the examples in Table 1.

TABLE 1 Formal vs. Informal Present Tense Endings

Language	Formal *you*	Informal *you*
Spanish	*[usted] habla* (you speak) *[usted] come* (you eat)	*[tu] hablas* (you speak) *[tu] comes* (you eat)
Japanese	*hanashimasu* (you speak) *tabemasu* (you eat)	*hanasu* (you speak) *taberu* (you eat)
French	*vous parlez* (you speak) *vous mangez* (you eat)	*tu parles* (you speak) *tu manges* (you eat)

English verbs do not operate in a similar way, so ESL students who are trying to translate "formality" through grammatical endings will have a perplexing time. Not only does English not have a grammatical solution to this problem, it actually requires learners to know multiple labels or vocabulary for the very same social function. Consider the word that means to "to get rid of something, especially something that is viewed as useless or unpleasant." The word that the learner is looking for is *discard*, yet in natural conversation, we do not use this word. Instead, we use the phrasal verb *throw away*, which sounds more conversational than the more formal *discard*, just as *put up with* is easier on the ears than *tolerate*.

A third difficulty of phrasal verbs is that they are often reduced in conversation. Thus, they are not only hard to comprehend semantically, they are simply hard to hear. Consider this conversation:

> *A:* What did you **think of** the test?
> *B:* I thought it was kind of tough, especially the last part.

> *A:* Yeah, it was. Hey, did you **come up with** a good answer for the essay question?
> *B:* At first, no, but then I started writing down a few things, and then the answer just sort of **took off**.

An ESL student would have a hard time hearing the pieces of each of these phrasal verbs. In *think of*, the word *of* is greatly reduced as is *with* in *come up with*. In the example *took off*, the two words get run together so that they sound much more like "to cough" than *took* and *off*. If—**and this is a huge assumption that should never be underestimated**— the student has actually been able to accurately hear the phrasal verb and caught all the pieces, then the learner still faces the semantic challenge: What does it mean? This is further complicated in conversation because the conversation keeps flowing as the learner is still trying to decipher the phrasal verb, and more phrasal verbs are bombarding him or her.

The fourth problem of phrasal verbs is the particle or preposition. This added part is actually critical to meaning because it is what differentiates *postpone* (*put off*) from *get dressed* (*put on*) or *solve a problem* (*come up with*) from *get sick* (*come down with*). Phrasal verbs can be separable or nonseparable. For example, we can say, "The teacher *called off* the test," but we can also say, "The teacher *called* the test *off*." Either of these is correct. In the first example, the ESL learner is lucky in that the pieces of the phrasal verb are next to each other. However, in the second example, the word *off*, which is crucial to the meaning of *call off*, is actually three words away.

As if that were not complicated enough, English actually allows the particle to "float" much more than three words away. Consider this conversation involving the phrasal verb *look up*, meaning to search for information in a book or other source:

A: Did you do the homework?

B: What homework?

A: Well, we were supposed to *look* all those Latin and
    Greek roots on page 52 *up*.

B: Are you serious? I forgot!

In this example, *up* is located ten words away from *look*. This kind of structure happens frequently in conversation and is yet another example of why phrasal verbs are difficult vocabulary for ESL learners.

Idioms

All languages feature idiomatic expressions, and each idiomatic expression, or idiom, is a vocabulary item. The test of whether a "chunk" is an idiom or not is whether the sum of the meanings of the individual words is equal to or similar to the meaning of the whole phrase.

Most phrasal verbs, for example, are idiomatic. As explained earlier, *throw up* is not the sum of *throw* and *up*. ESL learners are confused when they find out that the opposite of *put on* clothing is not *put off* clothing. If removing clothing is to *take off* clothing, then why isn't the opposite *taking on* clothing? With idioms, logic often has no place.

When a person *lets the cat out of the bag*, there is no cat, there is no bag, and there is no cat in any bag. The words *let, cat, out,* and *bag* are all frequent words, ones that might be covered in any basic or even beginning-level English class. However, knowing the meaning of these four words hardly prepares the learner to figure out the meaning of this idiom. Other idioms include *raining cats and dogs, feeling blue, sell like hotcakes, jump the gun, be up in the air, get with it, shake a leg, a feather in one's cap, wake up on the wrong side of the bed,* and *have a bad hair day.*

The best work on identifying which idioms are used in spoken American English was done by Liu (2003), who examined three corpora containing a total of six million words. The composite list contains three bands according to the usage. Here are the top 15 idioms (in order of frequency) from Band 1, the most frequently used idioms in spoken American English: *kind of, sort of, of course, in terms of, in fact, deal with, at all, as well, make sure, go through, come up, look for, find out, go on,* and *as well as.* It is easy to see that these examples are idioms because they do not mean what they would appear to mean—that is, their literal meaning is not being used. For example, *kind* as a noun means "type" or "class." However, consider the literal and idiomatic meanings of *kind of* here:

Literal: *The cobra is a kind of snake.*
Idiomatic: *It's kind of hot today, isn't it?*

PART II: What Does It Mean to Know a Word? What Does Knowing a Word Include?

When you ask a student, "Do you know this word?" and the student says, "Yes," what proof would convince you that the student does indeed know the word? More than likely, the answer is the meaning of the word. To answer the question, "Do you know this word?" we expect a student to provide the meaning. However, knowing a word involves much more than knowing just its meaning.

Polysemy

First of all, a word rarely has just one meaning. Most words in English are polysemous, that is, they have multiple meanings. Some have relatively few meanings. For example, *shovel* can be the instrument or the action. (This may not seem like two things to you, but note how we shovel with a shovel, mop with a mop, and mow with a mower, but we sweep with a broom, paint with a brush, and charge with a card.)

With a relatively small number of meanings, *shovel* is clearly in the minority in English. *Table* can be the piece of furniture, a set of numbers or figures, the action of not talking about something in a meeting, or a descriptive word (as in table scraps or tablecloth). Other words have multiple meanings: *put, put on, put down, put off, put away, put up with, put back*, etc.

An example that the students like to confront us with is *get*, so it behooves teachers to become very familiar with this verb. Consider how the meaning of *get* changes so dramatically in these examples: *get mail* (receive without trying), *get the mail* (go to a place to retrieve it), *get the measles* (contract a sickness), *get angry* (become), *get to the airport* (arrive), *get in a car* (enter), *get washed* (passive voice), and many others.

Connotation

All words have a denotation and a connotation. The denotation refers to the most basic or specific meaning of a word. In contrast, a connotation is an idea that is suggested by or associated with a word. For example, the word *scum* is just the name of a layer that forms on the surface of a body of water, but the word has connotations of impurity, badness, and ugliness.

Table 2 illustrates denotation and connotation of five words that express a similar concept.

While denotation is fairly straightforward, connotation can vary. The connotation of a word can change from negative to positive or vice-versa over time. The connotation of a word can also vary from culture to culture (even with two cultures or groups that speak the same language) as well as from individual to individual. The connotations listed in Table 2, for example, are the connotations that I, based on my life experiences, would assign to these words. To me, *thin* is a neutral word. To some, hearing "You look so thin!" would be a positive statement, while to others it would be a negative statement. To me, *skinny* has a neutral to negative connotation. *Slim* seems to be more positive when it deals with weight. (In contrast, in the phrase *slim chance*, it has a negative connotation, but that is a different meaning.) *Lean* and *slender* have positive connotations, which explains why weight loss or nutrition companies have chosen these words for their brand names (e.g., Lean Cuisine®).

Connotation can also impact a nonnative speaker's ability to learn a new vocabulary item since the positive or negative value assigned to a word by the learner also plays a role in how difficult a word is to learn. Positive words are easier to remember than negative words (Ludwig, 1984). In two empirical studies (Yavuz, 1963; Yavuz & Bousfield, 1959), English-speaking individuals learned translations of 18 Turkish words equally divided into positive, neutral, and negative words. In both

TABLE 2 Denotation vs. Connotation

Word	Denotation	Connotation
thin	not overweight	neutral image
skinny	not overweight	negative image
slim	not overweight	positive image
lean	not overweight	positive image
slender	not overweight	positive image

experiments, recall was significantly better for the positively loaded words than for the neutral or negative words. The teaching principle here is that words that have (or seem to have—to the learner at least) a negative connotation may be more difficult to commit to memory.

Spelling and Pronunciation

English is a language that has a relatively low letter-to-sound correlation, thus making many English words difficult to spell and/or pronounce (from the written letters). This is especially true when English is compared with languages such as Japanese or Spanish where pronunciation is consistent with the way words are spelled.

Knowing the spelling of a word is in itself quite an accomplishment for a nonnative speaker. Consider the sound /i/ (*ee* in some dictionaries). This one sound can be written in at least eight different ways: **eat**, n**ee**d, retr**ie**ve, p**eo**ple, k**ey**, rec**ei**ve, b**e,** laz**y**. Likewise, knowing the correct pronunciation can be problematic. The letter *a* can be pronounced in at least five ways: *cat* /ae/, *father* /a/, *lawn* /[ɔ]/, *cake* /eI/, *interval* /ə [schwa]/.

Part of Speech

Knowing the part of speech of a word is important. It is important when learners know two or more forms for one word: *wise* (adj.), *wisely* (adv.), *wisdom* (n.). It is also important when similar words confound the situation: *lend* (v.) vs. *loan* (n.) or *affect* (v.) vs. *effect* (n.).

The part of speech of a word can make a word harder to master. "Psychological research shows differential performance on tasks involving nouns, verbs, adjectives, and adverbs, indicating that the form class of a word is a reasonably potent variable in verbal tasks" (Ludwig, 1984, p. 554). While the exact ranking of the parts of speech in terms of difficulty is not clear, Laufer (1990) sums it up best: "It is sometimes argued that certain grammatical categories are more difficult to learn than others. Nouns seem to be the easiest; adverbs—the most difficult; verbs and adjectives—somewhere in between" (p. 298). In follow-up interviews of learners using the keyword method, Atkinson (1975) found similar results. Learners reported that the keyword method worked best for nouns, less well for verbs, and least well for adjectives. Phillips (in Laufer, 1990) noted an interaction between the effect that part of speech has on word difficulty and the proficiency level that a learner has: nouns were easier to learn than verbs or adjectives, an effect that decreased as the learner's proficiency increased.

Abstract words seem to be more difficult than concrete words. According to Mackey (1965), the reason that nouns are easier to remember than verbs or adjectives is probably a function of concreteness and of frequency. Laufer (1990) cautions, however, that "if all the other features of two words were identical, the concrete one would probably be easier. In the real learning situation, however, many concrete words present a problem since they may contain other factors of difficulty" (p. 300).

Some teachers may assume that once a learner knows one of the basic four forms of a word (i.e., noun, verb, adjective, adverb), the learner either knows or easily learns all four forms. This is not the case. In a study of 106 undergraduate and graduate nonnative English–speaking students, Schmitt and Zimmerman (2002) found that it was rare for a student to know all four forms or no form of a word. In other words, partial knowledge of at least one form was the norm. Results also showed that learners tended to have a better understanding of the noun and/or verb forms rather than the adjective and/or adverb forms. The authors conclude that teachers cannot assume that learners will absorb the derivative forms of a word family automatically from exposure and suggest explicit instruction in this area of vocabulary.

Frequency

Knowing a word can also mean that the learner knows the frequency of occurrence of that word. Though this aspect of a word may seem almost trivial, the frequency of a word is often cited as a major factor in a given word's difficulty. In fact, Haynes (1993) claims that word frequency is probably *the* major component in word difficulty.

A given word may well express the concept that the person wants to express; however, that concept may have several possible names, some of which may be more useful to a nonnative learner because that particular word is more frequent. The rarer forms, though most certainly semantically appropriate, would make the speaker sound strange.

Complete this sentence with a word that means that you are extremely hungry: "I'm _____." Many people would complete the sentence with the word *starving*, but words such as *ravenous* and *famished* are certainly possible. However, *ravenous* and *famished* are not nearly as common as *starving*. Likewise, while *violet* and *purple* may refer to the same color, the latter is used much more frequently, so a nonnative learner should also use *purple* more often than *violet*. Using the word *violet* when the vast majority of native speakers would say *purple* would "mark" the learner's English as non-native.

Usage

Knowing a word also means knowing when it is appropriate to use that word instead of a synonym or similar word. This information about usage can include both syntactic information (e.g., we hardly ever use this verb in passive voice) and pragmatic information (e.g., we do not use this word when speaking to people of higher status). For example, the words *thing* and *stuff* are similar in meaning, but one is considered a standard word while the other is considered slang or informal language. The first word would be considered acceptable to use in, say, a job interview, but the second one would probably not.

Let us consider the concept of "not continue to live." The basic vocabulary item to express this concept is the word *die*. At the same time, let us consider differences in usage of three other vocabulary items that express the same denotation.

We can say, "I'm sorry to hear that your mother died," but it might be more common, especially when talking with a known person and wishing to convey our sympathy, to say, "I'm sorry to hear that your mother passed away." Thus, the usage of *pass away* may be restricted to a speaker who knows the listener and who wishes to express sincere regret or sympathy. That same person could not say, "I'm sorry to hear that your mother kicked the bucket" or "I'm sorry to hear that your mother is pushing up daisies."

The vocabulary item *kick the bucket* is often used for a deceased person that we did not know or did not care for much. Thus, there is a pragmatic/sociolinguistic usage issue with this vocabulary item. In addition, there is a syntactic issue with *kick the bucket*. In the example of SUBJECT + *kick* + *the bucket*, the subject must be a person or living thing, *kick* would be a transitive verb, and *the bucket* would be the object of the verb. Thus, *kick* is in the active voice. Any verb in the active voice can also be used in the passive voice. Consider, however, the usage problems associated with this particular vocabulary item in these two examples:

1. The old man kicked the bucket last week. (active voice)
2. The bucket was kicked by the old man last week. (passive voice)

In Sentence 1, active voice, the meaning could be literal (the old man really did use his foot to kick the bucket) or it could be figurative/idiomatic (the old man died). In Sentence 2, passive voice, the meaning can only be the literal meaning that the old man actually *kicked* the bucket. Therefore, in terms of usage, this particular idiom cannot be used in passive voice. This is a special usage issue for this vocabulary item since all active voice verbs should be able to be transformed to a passive voice form as well.

Similarly, the vocabulary item *push up daisies* has several special usage issues. Syntactically, *push up daisies* would appear to be a simple V + O construction. Given that *push* is a verb, we could in theory use this verb in any of the 12 different verb tenses. However, the verb in this vocabulary item is rarely used in any tense except a future progressive construction with *going to* or with *will*: He**'s going to be pushing** up daisies. He**'ll be pushing** up daisies. This expression does not occur in simple past tense even though *die* is frequently used in the past tense: He **pushed** up daisies vs. He **died**. Another syntactic usage issue is that this expression, similar to what we saw with *kick the bucket*, occurs only in active voice, never in passive voice. We cannot say even in future progressive tense, "Daisies will be being pushed up by him."

This vocabulary item also has a pragmatic/sociolinguistic usage limitation. At a register level, we could say that *kick the bucket* and *push up daisies* are slang or informal language while *die* and *pass away* are standard words. A nonnative learner could easily assume—albeit incorrectly—that the two slang expressions could be used interchangeably, as could the two standard vocabulary items. Natural usage of *push up daisies* is in situations involving a warning of an impending death for a certain reason. Consider this example: *He'll be pushing up daisies if he testifies against us.*

Collocation

Perhaps the single most important aspect of knowing a word for nonnative learners—besides or in addition to the obviously requisite synonym or denotation meaning—is the collocation(s) of a new vocabulary item. The meaning of collocation is apparent in its constituent parts: **co** (together) + **location** (place). A **collocation** is a word or phrase that naturally and frequently occurs before, after, or very near the target vocabulary item.

Make a sentence in your head with the word *squander*, which means to waste or use unwisely. (Do not go on without coming up with an example!) In theory, any noun could follow the word *squander*, but the most common collocations for squander in English are *money* or *resources* (salary, $1,000, or inheritance), *time* (the morning, her vacation, a lifetime), or *opportunity* (opportunity, chance, prospect). Thus, common collocations for the verb *squander* are money, time, and opportunity.

Consider the vocabulary item *commit*. *Commit* has three different meanings: (1) make or do, (2) dedicate resources, or (3) be dedicated to, always used in the passive voice. One could argue that these are three different words, so we will work with the first meaning only, which is "to make or do." Complete this sentence: *He committed* _____.
What are some examples that pop into your head right away?

The most common collocations for *commit* as a verb are all types of crimes: *commit murder, commit suicide, commit grand larceny, commit adultery.* Thus, *commit* does not mean just "do or make" but "do or make something negative." An ESL student who learns that *commit* in *commit a murder* means "to do or perform an action" might attempt to make the following seemingly logical combinations: *commit a joke on someone, commit the housework, commit a lie.* The problem—a huge problem for nonnative learners—is that *commit* does not collocate with *joke, housework,* or *lie.*

The most common vocabulary items collocate with all sorts of words. The rarer the vocabulary word is (i.e., more likely to be an "advanced" word for a second language learner), the fewer the collocations will be. The verb *take* can collocate with *a taxi, a shower, medicine, a test, a person from one place to another, someone's temperature, a credit card*, and on and on. In fact, the verb *take* derives its meaning from its object collocation. On the other hand, a rarer word such as *exempt* has more specific collocations. In the active voice, the word following *exempt* will almost always be a person. The next collocation slot will be the word *from*. The third collocation slot will be some sort of requirement. The collocation patterns for the word *exempt* are illustrated here:

Collocations for *EXEMPT*				
(subject)	**exempt** (all verb tenses possible)	(someone)	*from*	a requirement a test taking the test having to get a passport

Certain target vocabulary can have rather complex collocations, and knowing which words can be used with the new word can make that word (even) more difficult for L2 learners. Collocations may vary greatly from language to language and may therefore not be transferred from L1 to L2. Because of both the difficulty and the importance of collocations (Nattinger & DeCarrico, 1992), McCarthy (1994) advocates direct instruction and practice in this area.

What obviously then follows from this is, how can teachers know which words collocate with a certain vocabulary item? The first answer is to trust your intuition as a native speaker. What would you say in this particular example? Make up a sentence in your head, but remove yourself from any classroom or ESL setting. How do you think a native speaker would *naturally* use that word? If you are a nonnative speaker, trust your knowledge of English. You have attained a certain level of knowledge of English, and you most likely know what combines with what.

A second solution is to use data from corpus linguistics. A corpus is a set or body of language examples such as actual newspapers, books, transcripts of conversations or interviews, or movie scripts. All of the corpus becomes the source or databank from which collocation software is used to identify collocations. For example, if we did a search for the word convey, we might find these examples:

. . . he said. I think he wanted to *convey* the message that there is hope that . . .

. . . do you think is the best way to *convey* this information? Is it that we are . . .

. . . Wilson had failed to accurately *convey* what the Prime Minister said. An . . .

. . . say they rely on Mr. Sims to *convey* messages that they do not want . . .

. . . public demonstrations does not *convey* a message independently of the . . .

This is but a small example, but we can see that *convey* frequently collocates with the word *message*. Other collocations for convey are *information* and *what (someone) say/says/said*. This information is important so that teachers do not tell students that *convey* means "send" but rather that *convey a message* means to *send a message*. From this students can then understand that *convey information* means to *send information*. The teaching point here is to teach the collocation, not just the meaning of one of the words in isolation when in fact that word does not usually occur alone? (When is the last time you said, "Yes, I'll convey that to you tomorrow"? Never!)

What Does All of This Mean?

What we have seen so far is that vocabulary in any language is a complex issue. In ESL terms, there are many kinds of vocabulary. Most people think of only single words. To be sure, these are numerous and problematic for our learners, but there are many other kinds of vocabulary that present additional and important challenges. We have also seen that knowing a word is not nearly as straightforward as it may have seemed. Is knowing a synonym sufficient? Is translating enough? Is the ability to use the word in a sentence enough? The important point as we look at the eight myths presented in this book is that a word is not just a single word and that knowing a word is actually a multipart task.

In learning another language, vocabulary is not as important as grammar or other areas.

In the Real World . . .

IN 1988, I TOOK A JOB TEACHING ENGLISH at a university in Urasa, a small, rural town in Niigata Prefecture in Japan. It was so rural at that time that Urasa had only two food stores, both extremely small.

If you've ever lived abroad for any extended period, you know that there often comes a time when all you can think about is a certain kind of food or drink that reminds you of home—even if you rarely, if ever, ate this food when you were home. Well, I grew up in south Louisiana and Mississippi, and for whatever reason, on my third day in this tiny town in rural Japan, I *had* to have homemade biscuits. Never mind that I hardly ever ate biscuits growing up. That was not the point. I just *had* to have home-made biscuits.

To accomplish this culinary objective, I went to one of the small stores to buy flour, the one biscuit ingredient that I did not yet have in my apartment. Before coming to Japan, I had been teaching in Malaysia. There I took a short course in basic Japanese so that I would have some communicative ability in my new teaching country. Because this was the sixth language that I had studied (after French, Spanish, Arabic, Malay, and German), I was familiar with basic language courses and what you need to be able to say to function in a foreign language setting. In my basic Japanese class, we studied two of the "alphabets" (hiragana and katakana), some basic expressions, and some basic grammatical patterns. As I was on my way to the store, I thought about what language I would need to buy flour, and my brain focused in on the basic pattern of, "*Sumimasen.* _____-*wa doko desu ka*" or "Excuse me, where is the _____?"

I felt quite confident on this shopping mission: I had the basic grammar that I needed, and after all, I knew what flour looked like and I knew that the store was quite small, so how hard could this be? Well, in hindsight, even with some basic grammar knowledge, I was quite ill prepared.

When I entered the tiny store, two petite, demure older women bowed and bowed and bowed as they greeted me, "Welcome. Welcome to our store." I could tell that they did not speak a word of English, but that did not matter because I knew the grammar pattern that I needed for this purchase, and I knew how to bow and smile and be polite. What could go wrong?

After the greeting, I set out to find a small bag of flour. I remember thinking that I should look for a small paper bag with two gold sheaths of wheat on the front of the bag—reminiscent of the brands of flour that I remembered seeing in kitchens in my past. Within five minutes, I had scoured the whole tiny store and found no such bag or anything similar. What I did find was a section with several clear plastic bags with different kinds of powdered items in them. The problem: I couldn't read the kanji (the Chinese characters) or understand the words written in hiragana on them (though I could pronounce these aloud because hiragana is phonetically transparent). Was this powder in the bag flour? Or corn starch? Or baking soda? Or even powdered milk? Or perhaps some other more exotic Japanese food product?

The store was empty except for me, and the two women were carefully eyeing this "lost" foreigner in their store. I was no threat, but I must have looked confused to them. I kept walking to the bread section (I could recognize bread in these bags!) and tried to compare the written word for bread in Japanese (*pan*, from Portuguese) with the characters written on the other bags of powdered goods.

Unable to locate the main ingredient for making biscuits, I finally decided to ask the women for help. "Excuse me," I began. Then I realized that I did not have any idea how to say *flour* in Japanese. Being a good language learner, I tried to circumvent this by mentally going through possible strategies: a synonym, a definition, an explanation, a drawing. All of these were problematic. I don't know of a synonym for flour in English, let alone Japanese. I didn't have the vocabulary for a definition or an explanation either. I couldn't draw flour.

As the women stared at me, I said in Japanese, "I want bread. I eat bread." With that, we all looked at the lovely loaves of bread not ten feet from us. I then used my knowledge of grammar to say, "No, not bread. Before bread." If you know anything about the study of Japanese as a Second Language, you know that for a beginning Japanese learner to correctly use the prepositional phrase "before bread" is actually quite a feat since prepositions in Japanese go *after* the noun and require a special grammatical marker. *"Pan no mae ni"* came out of my mouth effortlessly because I knew my grammar. Unfortunately, they were as confused by "before bread" as a native English speaker would be if I had delivered this message in English. It just didn't make sense.

By sheer coincidence, one of my English students was walking in front of the store at that very moment. I ran outside and shouted to him as he was crossing the street, "How do you say *flour* in Japanese?" He answered, "*Hana*," and armed with this valuable piece of information, I rushed up to the women and smilingly and in my best, most polite Japanese said, "*Sumimasen. Hana-wa doko desu ka*" (Excuse me. Where is the *hana*?)

The women smiled, and I could see their sense of relief that the foreigner was about to make a purchase and actually leave them in peace. I, too, was ready to get this ordeal over with and make the biscuits. Unfortunately, my joy was shortlived as the happy women led me to the produce section.

It took me a minute to understand what had happened. There in front of us were several carefully wrapped clear plastic packages of beautifully arranged yellow chrysanthemums. Yes, they were flowers. When I asked my student for the Japanese word for flour, I had not specified whether I meant *flour* or its homonym *flower*, and since *flower* is a more common word than *flour*, my student told me *hana* instead of *komugi*. (Now I know!) Compounding this linguistic confusion was the fact that people in Japan do actually eat flowers in their salad, so they are sold as food products in stores.

Needless to say, I did not get the flour and I was unable to make biscuits on my third evening in Japan. It is important to note that all of my grammar knowledge—plus the fact that I was actually able to re-trieve it and use it correctly in a "real" situation—was of little to no help to me. What I needed in that situation was one word: *komugi*. In this experience, I learned that vocabulary is actually **more important** than grammar.

This is not to say that I want to end up speaking Japanese in Tarzan-like delivery, but this is a real example of where vocabulary knowledge would have gotten me what I wanted/needed more than any grammar knowledge.

What the Research Says . . .

Learning a second language entails learning numerous aspects of that language, including vocabulary, grammar, pronunciation, composi-tion, reading, culture, and even body language. Unfortunately, tradi-tionally vocabulary has received less attention in second language (L2) pedagogy than any of these other aspects, particularly grammar. Arguably, vocabulary is perhaps *the* most important component in L2 ability. For more than 2,000 years, the study of a foreign language pri-marily entailed grammatical analysis, which was practiced through translation of written work (Hinkel & Fotos, 2002). As a result, vocab-ulary has been academically excluded from or at best limited within L2 curricula and classroom teaching. A perusal of ESL textbooks quickly reveals a lack of focus on vocabulary. Unlike books in French, Spanish, or other foreign languages, there are no vocabulary lists in the lessons/units or vocabulary index at the back of the book. Exercises practicing vocabulary may be found in reading books, but such exercises are rarely found in grammar books, speaking books, listening books, or writing books in spite of the importance of vocabulary in these areas. Language programs might have a grammar class or a reading class, but there is almost never a vocabulary class. For far too long, it has been incorrectly assumed that learners will pick up enough vocabulary without direct instruction.

One of the first observations that second language learners make in their new language is that **they need vocabulary knowledge** to function well in that language. How frustrating it is when you want to say something and are stymied because you don't know the word for a simple noun! In spite of the obvious importance of vocabulary, most courses and curricula tend to be based on grammar or a combination of grammar and communication strategies rather than vocabulary. As a result, even after taking many courses, learners still lack sufficient vocabulary knowledge. Vocabulary knowledge is critical to any communication. Wilkins (1972) summarizes the situation best: "While without grammar very little can be conveyed, without vocabulary *nothing* can be conveyed" (p. 111).

Adult L2 learners are painfully aware of their plight. They see acquisition of vocabulary as their greatest source of problems (Green & Meara, 1995; Meara, 1980). In end-of-course surveys of ESL students in intensive academic programs (Flaitz, 1998; James, 1996; Folse 2004b), students expressed a strong desire for vocabulary instruction. In fact, when asked what could improve the ESL programs in which they were studying, students ranked "more vocabulary development" second only to "more opportunities to speak in class." Clearly, L2 learners know that vocabulary is critical to L2 success, and they consistently cite their lack of vocabulary knowledge as an area in which they are deficient. This is problematic because, as Meara (1980) notes, second language "learners themselves readily admit that they experience considerable difficulty with vocabulary, and once they have got [*sic*] over the initial stages of acquiring their second language, most learners identify the acquisition of vocabulary as their greatest single source of problems" (p. 221). These learners know that vocabulary is important; think about it: they do not carry grammar books with them but dictionaries (Krashen, 1989).

Richards (1976) notes that the "teaching and learning of vocabulary have never aroused the same degree of interest within language teaching as have such issues as grammatical competence, contrastive analysis, reading, or writing" (p. 77). This is not so surprising given the fact that vocabulary has not held as high a position in second language teaching and research as other language areas have. In the audio-lingual method, teachers led students through drills of structures, with clear emphasis on grammatical structures over vocabulary, which served merely to fill in the slots in the drills. In more recent communicative methods, emphasis was placed on communicating meaning. While grammar was not emphasized as much anymore, vocabulary was still relegated to a step-child position in language study. Since grammar has been viewed as more important than vocabulary, it follows that a great deal more research on grammar exists than does for the lexicon. In the various debates that have raged over direct versus indirect approaches, or over grammatical versus notional-functional syllabi, or over explicit instruction versus natural acquisition, the focus was almost always on the grammatical structures of the L2. Vocabulary was not emphasized; in fact, it was hardly ever an issue. (The lone notable exception here is Michael Lewis's attempts [1993, 1997] to move the field toward vocabulary with his lexical approach.)

Vocabulary is a key component of reading ability. Numerous researchers (Alderson, 1984; Beck, Perfetti, & McKeown, 1982; Coady, Magoto, Hubbard, Graney, & Mokhtari, 1993; Davis, 1944; Haynes, 1993; James, 1996; Kameenui, Carnine, & Freschi, 1982; Laufer, 1992, 1997; Nation & Coady, 1988) have shown the relationship between L2 vocabulary knowledge and L2 reading ability. Discussing a cognitive model of strategies that L2 learners make use of when they attempt to infer an unknown word's meaning, Huckin and Bloch (1993) point out, "Research has shown that second-language readers rely heavily on vocabulary knowledge, and that a lack of vocabulary knowledge is the largest obstacle for second-language readers to overcome" (p. 154). Likewise, Haynes and Baker (1993) found that the main obstacle for L2 readers is not lack of reading strategies but rather insufficient vocabulary knowledge in English. Laufer and Sim (1985) list these areas in order of decreasing importance in reading ability in L2: knowledge of vocabulary, subject matter, discourse markers, and syntactic structure. In sum, Laufer and Sim find that vocabulary is **most** important, syntax **least** important.

In addition, studies have shown the effect that a large L2 vocabulary base can have on writing skills (Laufer & Nation, 1995; Laufer, 1998b) and in listening and speaking tasks (Joe, 1995; Joe, Nation, & Newton, 1996; Newton, 1995). While correlation does not necessarily imply causality, the fact is that empirical studies have shown that good L2 readers, writers, speakers, and listeners have a more extensive vocabulary under their control.

Following Krashen's influential writings (1982, 1989, 1993), many L2 programs adopted a curriculum that limits or excludes explicit instruction in any aspect of L2, including vocabulary. With the goal of focusing on providing *comprehensible input*, these programs primarily make use of communicative activities without explicit instruction in either vocabulary or grammar. (This philosophy appears to be somewhat in flux.) In other programs, grammar remains the primary focus of the curriculum. This lack of attention to vocabulary is most unfortunate for L2 learners, for as Lewis (1993) points out: "Language consists of grammaticalised lexis, not lexicalised grammar." Without grammar, little communication may be possible; without vocabulary, **no** communication is possible.

As more and more empirical research in L2 is made available and results provide important insight into our questions about vocabulary learning and teaching, the education pendulum is swinging back toward some more "traditional" methods, including those that rely on explicit instruction from the teacher. This in turn begs the question of what kinds of classroom activities, especially vocabulary activities, are effective for L2 learners. Carter and McCarthy (1988) conclude that

> although it suffered neglect for a long time, vocabulary
> pedagogy has benefited in the last fifteen years or so from

theoretical advances in the linguistic lexicon, from psycholinguistic investigations into the mental lexicon, from the communicative trend in teaching, which has brought the learner into focus, and from developments in computers. What is perhaps missing in all this is more knowledge about what happens in classrooms when vocabulary crops up. (p. 51)

In a study of French immersion classes in Canada, Clipperton (1994) noted that his students had an acute problem with vocabulary. He went on to lament, however, that the emphasis in second language classroom instruction continues to be on syntax. This emphasis on grammar is surprising in current pedagogy that focuses on comprehensible input and communicative activities because people can generally communicate their meaning with less than perfect grammar whereas incorrect use of vocabulary can substantially impede communication.

Echoing these sentiments, Maiguashca (1993) noted that the role that vocabulary has played has been secondary, serving only to fill illustrations of grammar points. One possible reason for the inferior status of vocabulary vis-à-vis grammar is that language teachers themselves do not view vocabulary as being that complicated a matter. In their thinking, learning vocabulary seems to be at most a matter of memorizing lists of words and their meanings. Oftentimes, vocabulary is seen as something that learners can pick up on their own as they continue to focus on grammar and sentence patterns. This view, however, is changing as more and more research into how learners acquire L2 vocabulary is being conducted (de Groot & Keijzer, 2000; Grace, 2000; Gu 2003; Hulstijn & Laufer, 2001; Kitajima, 2001; Sanaoui, 1995).

It is time for ESL educators to move our teaching, our curricula, and our materials beyond our traditional focus on grammar. This is *not* to say that we should abandon grammar. Certainly, structural patterns for the particular proficiency level of the learners will always be taken into account. However, L2 vocabulary research has entered a new phase in which we are no longer looking at whether vocabulary should be emphasized but rather what aspect of vocabulary teaching/learning we should be focusing on. Table 3 shows some of the variety in recent vocabulary research.

TABLE 3 Recent Areas of Second Language Vocabulary Research

How many words and which words do learners need to know?	Coxhead, 2000; Hazenberg & Hulstijn, 1996; Laufer, 1989
How do L2 learners' vocabularies develop?	de Groot & Keijzer, 2000; Hunt & Beglar, 1998; Jones, 1995; Kitajima, 2001; Laufer & Paribakht, 1998; Parry, 1993; Schmitt, 1998a, 1998b, 1998c; Schmitt & Zimmerman, 2002; Yu, 1996
Why are some words more difficult to learn than others?	Cooper, 1999; Ellis, 1994; Laufer, 1997; Nation, 2000; Tréville, 1996; Waring, 1997
Is L2 vocabulary learned more easily through natural context or through direct instruction?	Grace, 1998; Laufer & Shmueli, 1997; Mondria & Wit-de Boer, 1991; Prince, 1995; Schatz & Baldwin, 1986; Zahar, Cobb, & Spada, 2001; Zimmerman, 1997
Which vocabulary learning strategies do students employ?	Folse, 2003b; Gu, 1994; Gu & Johnson, 1996; Laufer & Yano, 2001; Lessard-Clouston, 1996; Morrison, 1996; Olsen, 1999; Sanaoui, 1995, 1996; Schmitt & Schmitt, 1993
Which types of practice activities promote vocabulary learning?	Folse, 1999b; Hulstijn & Laufer, 2001; Joe, 1998; Laufer & Hulstijn, 1998; Paribakht & Wesche, 1996, 1997, 1999; Snellings, van Gelderen, & de Glopper, 2002

What effect do certain types of marginal glosses and Internet annotations have on incidental vocabulary learning?	Al-Seghayer, 2001; Bell & LeBlanc, 2000; Chun & Plass, 1996; Duquette, Renie, & Laurier, 1998; Grace, 1998, 2000; Hulstijn, Hollander, & Greidanus, 1996; Laufer & Hill, 2000; Lomicka, 1998; Nagata, 1999; Roby, 1999; Watanabe, 1997
How does using a dictionary (or one type of dictionary) impact vocabulary acquisition?	Grace, 2000; Schatz & Baldwin, 1986; Tall & Hurman, 2000; Watanabe, 1997

As Table 3 clearly shows, research has investigated many areas of second language vocabulary learning and teaching. As a result, the question in L2 vocabulary teaching has shifted from if we should teach vocabulary to **when** and **how** we should be teaching vocabulary as well as **how much** and **which** vocabulary we should be working with. Teachers need to make vocabulary one of their primary course objectives. In addition, teachers should use both materials that emphasize vocabulary learning and let publishers know of their growing desire for more and better vocabulary materials. Publishers have been listening to these recent developments in the role of vocabulary in ESL, and a perusal of many ESL publishers' catalogs quickly bears this out. While grammar books and grammar-based materials are plentiful, vocabulary-focused materials are on the rise. A website search using the words "grammar" and "vocabulary" at three major ESL publishers found twice as many grammar books as vocabulary books at Heinle & Heinle (29 grammar to 14 vocabulary) but almost equal numbers at the University of Michigan Press (17 to 15) and Houghton Mifflin (13 to 11). Similar results were found for the total number of grammar books and vocabulary books at Alta and Delta, two distributors of different publishers' materials (as well as their own) for both ESL and foreign languages (407 grammar to 387 vocabulary).

What You Can Do . . .

1. Understand exactly how much of your students' ability to understand you is impacted by vocabulary issues.

This is a key issue for all language learners at all levels. For young learners, such as ESOL children in K–5 but also including all newcomers to public school who do not speak much English (or any English!), understanding their English-speaking teacher is going to depend heavily on body language (lots of smiles!), your patience and theirs, and vocabulary knowledge—your students' knowledge of English and your knowledge of how much vocabulary the students actually know (or do not know).

One of the most important things for these learners is comprehensible input. This means that you need to communicate with the students in language that is at their level and possibly a little beyond. This is what Krashen (1989) refers to as the *i + 1*, with *i* referring to the learner's current proficiency level and *+ 1* to a level just beyond the student's current ability in the new language.

If comprehensible input is so important, teachers need to know how to speak in "comprehensible input." In other words, how can you speak *i + 1*? First of all, **slow down**. Speak clearly. Instead of saying, "Whereya from?" or "Jeet lunch yet?" try to say all the words in a natural sounding way without skipping any—"Where are you from?" and "Did you eat lunch yet?" **Use simple vocabulary. Avoid phrasal verbs. Avoid idioms. Avoid slang**. When the student does not appear to understand, do not paraphrase at first. Try to say the exact same words to give the student a chance to understand what you said the first time. If your input does not appear to be comprehensible, then consider paraphrasing parts of your message the third or fourth time.

For those who are not so experienced with ESL students yet, consider watching the movie "Home Alone" (the original one, not part 2) again. This is an excellent movie for comprehensible input because the main character is lost and frequently asks questions such as, "Where am I?" and "Why? Why did my family forget me?" As he encounters adults who might endanger his cover, he often repeats their questions more slowly several times to buy time as he considers the best elusive answer to their questions. In addition to using a controlled vocabulary appropriate for young learners, the dialogue in this movie is well delivered by the actors. Their rate and pronunciation are on target for ESL learners even though this was not their goal.

2. Become more aware of the problem of vocabulary for our students.

It is important for all teachers to be aware of language problems that arise from lack of vocabulary knowledge. For those of you who have lived abroad for an extended period of time, you are well aware of the situations that your students are facing. For many learners, these problems range from not understanding a reading passage or part of a movie to not being able to express themselves accurately in writing or speaking because of too many unknown vocabulary words/items.

As you prepare a discussion activity, for example, it is imperative to consider not only the vocabulary in the *material* but also the vocabulary needed for the *task* itself. For example, let's suppose that your students are going to find out about a situation or topic and then discuss it to reach a consensus as to whether they agree on the topic or not. If you give them a copy of a newspaper article about the topic (reading) or if you put up an overhead transparency with information (reading) or if you tell them the information (listening), there may be vocabulary that the students do not know.

Consider this newspaper excerpt that a teacher took into her intermediate class to generate a discussion among her students, many of whom she knew to be avid baseball fans.

The Price of Baseball: Colorado Rockies Give in to Hickey's Contract Demands

The Colorado Rockies completed a deal with the Chicago White Sox for second baseman Jonathan Hickey early yesterday morning, according to the *Chicago Tribune*.

The Rockies agreed to ship their star pitcher to Seattle in a rather complex deal that also gave two minor leaguers as well as $8 million to the Chicago team. Sources familiar with the on-again, off-again contract negotiations confirmed that Rockies owner Kevin Lewis had spent weeks trying to resolve the issues of Hickey's contract perks, including the use of a chartered jet for the four-time All-Star and his wife.

Hickey agreed to waive his no-trade clause after the Rockies secured jet service under the terms of his staggering seven-year, $125 million contract and addressed a clause that grants him high-priced seats at games. As usual in these trades, team physicians must still exchange medical data before the commissioner's office can approve the trade.

The teacher knew that her students were very interested in baseball. She saw this short article (only 162 words) and copied it for her students to serve as a catalyst for a discussion. Her lesson plan revolved around these focal questions:

1. What is the main idea of this newspaper article?
2. Explain in your own words what the article says.
3. What is Hickey's new salary? What else did he receive?
4. What is your opinion of this salary package? Is this reasonable?

A quick read of the article and the teacher's four questions shows that the teacher wanted the students to talk about Hickey's salary package and whether or not this was reasonable. The purpose of this supposedly short reading was to give the students the facts about the case that they could then use in their discussion.

This article—even though it is short at 143 words—has more unknown vocabulary in it than the teacher realizes. A discussion cannot happen initially. Students will start asking vocabulary questions and/or they will take out their dictionaries to start looking up words. There are too many unknown but essential words in understanding not just the gist of the story but the nuances of what has happened. The second paragraph alone, with only 70 words, features these 12 unfamiliar words: *ship, rather, complex, deal, sources, on-again, off-again, negotiations, confirmed, resolve, issues, perks,* and *chartered.*

It is important for you to consider the amount of unknown vocabulary in this material. Some unknown vocabulary is not bad, but more than a few new words, especially if they are difficult words to understand, will detract from your task. Remember that the goal of this particular activity is speaking, not learning a lot of new vocabulary. If there are too many unknown words, you should not use this material. You should find a different source for the topic (use the Internet) or paraphrase the material.

You should make a list of the unknown vocabulary. At the very least, ask students if they know these words. You may wish to write them on the board. I prefer to have the words on a big piece of newsprint. This way the list can be put up and taken down and then put up again in a few days when I want to review the words—without my having to make a new list. (This is a real time-saver.)

So far, we have discussed the words contained in the material. This is the obvious vocabulary to consider, but there is another set of vocabulary that many teachers fail to consider: the vocabulary for the task.

If our topic is "Should the voting age be increased to 30?" we might run into words such as *vote, elect, due to, responsible, citizen, rights,* etc., in the material. However, these are not the words that you need for a general group discussion in which the task is to state your opinion, listen and react to others' opinions, and negotiate a consensus for the group. For this kind of task, speakers will need vocabulary such as: *I think that _____, I don't think that _____, Does anyone think that _____?, I agree with* (name). *Could you repeat that? Why do you think that? If you believe that, then what about _____? What about _____? No, how can you say that?* As you can see, this set of vocabulary is very different from the vocabulary in the material itself.

One vocabulary is content-related; the other is task-related. It is important that students know the material in both. Without this, the desired task is likely to flop.

3. Choose materials that emphasize vocabulary.

Choosing key vocabulary to be taught takes time. Designing proper written exercises to force students to retrieve newly learned vocabulary lesson after lesson takes extensive time. The problem: teachers do not have enough time.

Choose materials that emphasize vocabulary. There is no reason why you should add this to your already busy schedule. Why use materials that do not feature vocabulary lists or at the very least glossed or bolded words? Publishers can do this; they *will* do this if you tell them you want this. It is also important to have several exercises for students to practice new vocabulary. Since we know the importance of retrieval of new words, learners need exercises that not only promote but actually require learners to retrieve the form of the word or the meaning of the word. You want materials that have vocabulary presentation and vocabulary practice.

If you do not have a say in the textbook that you use, then try to find viable vocabulary websites that match the proficiency level of your students. One caveat worth noting here is that teachers must carefully evaluate the language level and intended audience (native or non-native speakers) of these websites. In this computer age, many students will gladly spend some time on Internet-based activities. If possible, choose sites that require students to enter their and your email address. In this way, you get a copy of your students' results as well as when they visited the site, how many times they visited, how long they stayed each time, and what score they got each time. Furthermore, students are aware that you will get a copy of this information, so they know that you are proclaiming loudly and clearly, "Vocabulary **is** important."

4. Include vocabulary on your quizzes and tests.

If you are teaching reading, it makes sense to include vocabulary on your quizzes or tests. However, vocabulary should be included in all quizzes and tests, not just reading. In a grammar test on negation, you could include these three new vocabulary words in this activity:

Grammar Quiz on Negation

1. "astronomy, biology, zoology: Why is *astronomy* different? Use *not* in your answer."

Student answer: <u>*Astronomy is different because it is not about animals.*</u>

A basic tenet of good testing is to test what you have taught in the way that it was taught. Teach interesting and relevant material in an interesting and relevant manner, and make students responsible for what you have taught. A test may be considered valid if it tests what was taught. Students need to see that *you,* as their language expert and input provider, value vocabulary. By including vocabulary on tests, you are sending a clear message that vocabulary is important and that students will be held accountable for their vocabulary learning. Your students will thank you!

2

Using word lists to learn second language vocabulary is unproductive.

AT A WORKSHOP IN JAPAN IN 1993, THE NOTED second language acquisition expert Rod Ellis asked the audience, which was composed of perhaps 90 percent Japanese EFL teachers and 10 percent English-speaking teachers, "I assume that most of you teachers here today learned English as a Foreign Language. What methods or techniques did your teachers use?" Most of the responses were murmurs of a few different methods, and then one older woman said in a somewhat shy voice but with impeccable English pronunciation, "Audiolingual."

Dr. Ellis's next question was addressed to this woman. "Do you think that was a good method? Was it effective?"

In typical Japanese fashion, she hesitated for a long time. She finally answered, "Well, I *thought* it was good," with emphasis on the word *thought* to indicate that she may have been wrong. In her voice— as we hear in many of our students' voices when we pose a difficult question to the entire group—you could hear that she was trying to give the right answer but hedge also. However, she really *did* think that audiolingual was a good way to learn English—at least for her. She put emphasis on the word *thought* to indicate that she expected Dr. Ellis's next comments to explain why audiolingual was bad since that is what the vast majority of current methods books tell us.

It is worth noting that the woman went on to describe how she had learned English, what it was like to do the drills, and how she had since gone on to become an English teacher. All of this was delivered in impeccable English. Dr. Ellis made a final comment that the audio-lingual method had clearly worked for her, and then he congratulated her on her excellent English.

This public display of not wanting to say the wrong thing—i.e., not wanting to say that the much maligned audiolingual method had in-deed been an effective way to learn English—is reminiscent of the tale of the emperor's new clothes. An idea takes hold, and then it is very hard to undo it or let it go. Learning vocabulary from lists fits in this category.

Millions of people learned languages from the grammar-translation method for many decades (and some still do!), and it featured lists of vocabulary. In addition, students taught via the natural approach were often given lists of key vocabulary. With the audiolingual method, em-phasis was on structured drills or patterns, but the words that learners had to substitute were often small lists of vocabulary. The vocabulary was not the target, but vocabulary lists were used nonetheless. In these methods, we can find learners who succeeded as well as those who did not. The point here is that no particular method or approach seems to have been that much more successful than another. Using lists appears to be neither detrimental nor miraculous.

There is little research to show that using lists actually hinders for-eign language learning. Like any other aspect of language teaching, it is but one tool that can be used to help learners learn. When I hear peo-ple blindly criticize vocabulary lists, I like to think back to the ex-change that I heard between Dr. Ellis and that English teacher in Japan.

What the Research Says . . .

In a nutshell, vocabulary lists are not "in," but we may be seeing a comeback now. This would certainly be good news for second language students, who need help in tackling the tremendous task of learning enough vocabulary to be able to communicate in their new language. Perhaps the worst that we can say about learning words from lists is that this activity is potentially dull (but effective). As a result, the big challenge in vocabulary teaching (and learning) is how to make this a pleasant activity given the large number of words to be learned (J. Hulstijn, personal communication, October 30, 1995).

In previous years, vocabulary texts contained lists of words that students were supposed to memorize and then be able to use when needed in communication. Reading passages and listening passages, for example, were sometimes preceded and/or followed by a list of words key to understanding the passage. These lists were in turn followed by exercises and activities of various kinds, but the format for the presentation of the words was a list.

When we talk about research on word lists in language teaching, it is important to make a distinction between research in which people memorize a list of known items and research in which people learn a list of new items. The latter is germane; the former is not. Many studies have looked at human ability to remember words in a list with the main focus being on how many words we can remember and how we can stretch this ability. The seminal work here is by Miller (1956), who found that adults, when given a list of items to attempt to memorize, have the ability to recall seven of the items—plus or minus two— without any special training. A logical follow-up question for psychologists was whether this ability could be improved. The answer is yes: by grouping the words into logical clusters, we are able to remember the groupings and, therefore, more items. Before we assume that there are implications from this for second language learning, let us examine this type of research more closely.

In this type of list-recalling activity, native speakers are given the task of remembering as many words as possible from a list of, say, 20 words within a specific, short time limit. Participants in Group A are given a randomized list of 20 words while participants in Group B are given the same 20 words but grouped semantically or morphologically, as illustrated in Table 4.

TABLE 4 List-Recall Words

Group A	Group B
spoon creation Toyota eaten	fork spoon knife eaten
creatively blue Ford fork	Toyota Ford Pontiac driven
green drawn create pencil	red blue green drawn
Pontiac paper knife driven	paper pencil ink written
ink red creative written	create creative creatively creation

Obviously, it is easier for us to remember more items from Group B than we can from Group A. This does not, however, tell us much about learning lists of foreign language vocabulary (for real purposes). In ESL and other language learning settings, we are much more interested in lists of *new and unknown* items that are followed by a synonym, a translation, or some notation to help the learner remember them.

Consider the task of an English-speaking student who is learning Japanese as a foreign language. The task is not to remember a list of known (English) items such as *pencil, car, green,* and *tree.* Nor is the task to remember a list of unknown (Japanese) words such as *empitsu, kuruma, midori,* and *ki.* Instead, the learner's task is to learn a list of unknown items that correspond to some known items. Such a list would look like this: *pencil = empitsu, car = kuruma, green = midori,* and *tree = ki.*

Another difference between the mental task with these two types of lists is that Miller and others looked at the effect of short-term memory of items. In real language teaching, however, we are more interested in learners' ability to retain these new words over time. Furthermore, the participants in this kind of psychological study had no real use or application for the material being memorized—that is, they were attempting to commit to memory a list of random words or numbers. In contrast, our students have a very different and real motivation because they will actually *use* this vocabulary.

Perhaps as a result of the more communicative approaches to language teaching, lists have fallen out of vogue. Learning from lists of decontextualized words was thought to not be valuable, so lists in textbooks disappeared. Commenting on vocabulary materials common in the 1980s and '90s, Maiguashca (1993) noted that "we have come a long way from the random, haphazard lists of L2 words, each accompanied by supposed L1 equivalents, which used to characterize language textbooks and manuals in the past" (p. 89). Yes, there was a change in how words were presented. Yes, the words were often accompanied by L1 equivalents, especially in foreign language materials or in EFL materials. However, the words were not haphazard—they were more often than not thematically related to the topic of the reading or listening passage.

While it is sometimes thought that learning words from lists is an ineffective way to learn new vocabulary, empirical evidence supporting this notion is scant. (How the words should be grouped and whether they should be accompanied by a translation are separate issues discussed in Myths 3 and 4, respectively.) In fact, Clipperton (1994) states that "it would appear that when new words are first presented, it may be best to do so out of context" (p. 743). Carter (1987) adds that while advanced learners may benefit from learning vocabulary in context, beginning learners probably benefit the most from words that are presented in lists of translation pairs. Carter and McCarthy (1988) note that research has made claims that translation pairs are not only useful but also that large quantities of new vocabulary can be learned efficiently and quickly in this way. Nation (1993) strongly advocates what he calls a "vocabulary flood" for beginning learners. This flood would invariably feature learning words from a list.

In a study of 128 Hebrew speakers studying EFL, Laufer and Shmueli (1997) compared four modes of presentation, including lists: (1) words presented in isolation, (2) words in minimal context (i.e., in one meaningful sentence) (3) words in text context, and (4) words in elaborated text context. In the isolated words condition, students were given a list of 20 words with L1 (first language) translations or English synonym equivalents. In the minimal context condition, students were given the same information as in (1) but with a single sentence of context. In the text condition, students read a passage that had all 20 target words with glosses in the margin. In the elaborated text condition, the material was the same text as in (3) but after lexical elaboration, thereby making the language, including the target words, more comprehensible. This last step represents what second language materials writers do with "real" material before adding it to their coursebooks.

In each mode, half of the target words were translated into the learners' L1 and the other half were explained in English. Words glossed in L1 were always retained better than words glossed in L2. As for the context effect, words presented in lists and in sentences were remembered better than words presented in text and elaborated text. Thus, in this study, *less* information was better. Retention scores were higher when less information or limited context was given about the word and lower when more information or extended context was given.

In another study, Prince (1995) examined the role of the L2 proficiency of learners and whether L2 vocabulary is presented in a list of L1 translations or in a series of L2 sentences (i.e., L2 context). Prince found that less proficient students were able to recall more items when they had learned the words in the translation condition rather than in the context condition. Thus, this research showed that some students perform better when they were given only a list of L2 words and their translations.

While lists may not be the most interesting way to present new vocabulary, the point here is that there is practically no evidence to suggest that learning new words in lists is in itself detrimental. One potential drawback heard from teachers is that students will gain only superficial knowledge of the new words. There is a concern that if students learn only the meaning as a translation or a simple synonym, then the students will not be able to actually use the word.

While this might initially appear to be a valid concern, learning a word is rarely a single off-on type of accomplishment, as we saw presented in the Introduction. Learning a word—that is to say, *knowing* a word—involves knowing many different kinds of things about that word. Thus, learning lists of words with a translation or with a synonym or simple definition can be seen as a solid first step. Once learners have a basic understanding of a word, they are then enabled to understand the word in passive encounters, such as in listening or reading, as well as use the word in the more active encounters in speaking and writing. (The terms *passive* and *active* as used here parallel Nation's [2001] use of *receptive* and *productive*.) At the very least, they are able to notice the word, and this attention aids in ultimate learning (Schmidt, 1990).

The argument that superficial learning of words in a list does not allow richer usage of the word—though intuitively appealing—does not hold up when we look at second language acquisition research. In Folse (1999b), I looked at the effect of exercise type on vocabulary retention (this will be discussed at length in Myth 8), but I also compared student production of new vocabulary, not just passive recognition. All of the target vocabulary words were presented in a list, and students were given specially written definitions, many of which were single-word synonyms or at best short definitions using very easy vocabulary. In the subsequent test of whether or not learners actually "knew" the word, learners had to demonstrate their knowledge by writing a definition or native language translation *and* a good example sentence using the word. While there was an effect for type of exercise, clearly learners were able to acquire words well enough to define them as well as use them in meaningful, original sentences.

If lists are not only acceptable but actually one of many useful tools in learning foreign language vocabulary, then this begs the question of which words should go in the lists. It is up to teachers to compile lists that are suitable for their students since no one is more familiar with the learning needs of a particular group of students than the teacher of that group. In addition, widely used word lists, usually targeting ESL students seeking to complete their tertiary studies in English, are available. In fact, several compilations are commonly used in materials and curriculum planning. These lists differ primarily in their intended learner audiences. These differences are outlined in Table 5.

TABLE 5 A Comparison of Word Lists

List	Words	Notes
teacher-generated	key vocabulary as chosen by the teacher or students	No one knows the students better than the teacher of those students.
Dolch List	220 sight words for elementary school children *(big, before, eight)*	• Prepared in 1936 • Based on frequency • Mostly function words; does not include concrete words • Useful in K–3 reading materials
General Service List	2,000 words that are of general service to learners *(the, city, prepare)*	• Published in 1953 • Based on frequency
University Word List	808 words that occur in academic text materials *(alternative, feasible, revive)*	• Published in 1984 • Based on frequency • Cover 8.5% of academic text words
Academic Word List	570 word families that occur in a variety of academic text materials *(consistent, aware, trigger)*	• Published in 1998 • Based on frequency • Only words that occur in many different types of academic material

As Table 5 indicates, the elementary school teachers have the Dolch List, which was prepared by E. W. Dolch in 1936. The words in this list are high-frequency words that make up from 50 to 75 percent of the reading material in English in U.S. elementary schools. Because these words are so important to basic reading, learners need to recognize them immediately; hence, they are often called **sight words**. These words cannot be learned through use of pictures (there are no concrete nouns on the list); children must be able to recognize these words at a glance before they can read confidently. By the end of third grade, all English-speaking students should be able to recognize the 220 words on the Dolch List.

The General Service List (West, 1953) is a list of 2,000 words whose frequency of occurrence make them of the greatest service to learners, hence the name for this list. Each word is followed by a number indicating the number of occurrences per five million words. The General Service List was widely used for years in designing content of graded readers and other learning materials. One problem with this list is the number of words. Each word has a headword and a list of its derivatives. For example, under the entry for *possession*, we find *possess* and *possessive*. Is this one word? Or three? And if it is three, is there one form that we should concentrate on? A more valid concern is the age of the words. Do these words reflect current usage?

Xue and Nation (1984) developed the University Word List (UWL), which is a list of about 800 vocabulary words that are common in academic texts. Academic texts were used as the data source because this list is designed to help nonnative speakers who are in an academic setting—that is, those who want to study in high school, community college, or university. This list does not include any of the words in the General Service List (GSL), so students should study the GSL before attempting the UWL. Nation (2000) estimates that this list covers 8.5 percent of academic texts. These words, though relatively few in number, are essential for learners to grasp the full meaning of an academic text.

More recently, Coxhead (2000) developed the Academic Word List (AWL), which consists of 570 word families. The selection process for these word families helped ensure a useful list of words. The words had to occur in over half of the 28 subject areas in the academic corpus of 3,500,000 words from which the word families were pulled. In addition, words had to occur more than 100 times in the corpus, and words had to occur at least ten times in each of the subject areas. These guidelines produced a list of words that are useful for the widest possible range of nonnative learners of English. Reflecting the academic nature of this list, the list does not include any of the word families occurring in the GSL.

Each of these lists is useful in its own right. What teachers must do is to see if one of these lists can be of assistance not only to the obvious needs of learners but to the often unnoticed need of teachers, who may want to use these lists in selecting words to teach or even to know which words to avoid using in their speech so as to make their speech more comprehensible for their learners. (In addition to these word lists, it is recommended that teachers take a look at the list of Liu's [2003] idioms commonly used in spoken American English.)

In conclusion, lists are not the evil that they have been portrayed to be. Research to support this claim of evil simply does not exist. In fact, many learners like learning from lists and actually ask for them. Therefore, it is important that teachers be aware of the various professionally developed lists that may (or may not) be appropriate for their particular students.

What You Can Do . . .

1. Don't hesitate to use vocabulary lists.

There is absolutely no reason not to present lists of words to your students provided that the words in the list are part of the regular curriculum. Hulstijn, Hollander, and Greidanus (1996) conclude that teachers should "give learners a list of important words for subsequent intentional learning, or, perhaps more motivating, encourage learners to draw up an individual list of words that they consider relevant to remember" (p. 337). (Words from lists can be used to create flashcards, a popular learning strategy that is discussed in greater detail on pp. 99–102.)

2. Don't rely only on word lists.

The problem here is not the particular method or teaching technique but rather the reliance to a large extent on *any* method or approach, including word lists (or drills or communicative speaking tasks). As with all things in life, moderation is the key. Good classroom teaching includes a variety of methods, approaches, and techniques to complement what is being taught and to whom it is being taught. Teaching ten concrete nouns to beginning learners might not be the same as teaching ten abstract nouns to advanced learners, so why would we use the same techniques?

3. Include your students' likes and dislikes as well as their classroom expectations in your teaching.

Despite what you have been told in training courses, many students **do** like lists. Lists are clear. Lists are concrete. Students can easily see what they know and what they do not know yet.

In some cultures, rote learning is the norm and students will expect this type of presentation of material. Good teaching is moving learners from point A to point Z. A good teacher can quickly "read" where the learners are initially. This involves knowing something about how they are accustomed to learning. When I taught in Saudi Arabia, my students loved lists. They asked for them, and when I gave them a list, I found that I could pretty much expect the majority of the students to know the words on that list within a few class meetings. Rather than working against your students' expectations, why not use them to the group's advantage?

3

Presenting new vocabulary in semantic sets facilitates learning.

In the Real World . . .

ALTHOUGH ALL OF 30 ESL TEXTBOOKS that I have authored over the years deal with vocabulary either directly or indirectly, about a dozen of these books are explicitly aimed at increasing ESL learners' base of known vocabulary: *Talk a Lot* (1993), *Beginning Reading Practices* (1997), *Discussion Starters* (1996), *Targeting Listening and Speaking* (with Bologna 2003), and *Intermediate Reading Practices, 3rd Ed.* (2004c). I have also designed vocabulary courses and worked on curricula at schools in several countries. In all of these projects, an important design question was how to organize the targeted vocabulary.

At some point, key vocabulary is identified; shortly thereafter, it has to be organized in some logical way. Sometimes we begin with key vocabulary and then seek to figure out a way to organize it. Sometimes we begin with pertinent topics, identify the relevant vocabulary, and then seek to figure out how to organize it. Other times we also identify language functions (e.g., describing people's physical traits), which produce key vocabulary necessary to complete these functions, and then seek how to organize the vocabulary.

As a materials writer and curriculum designer and even as a teacher, I have often wondered which way is the best way to organize the words. Is there a *best* way? Is there a *worst* way? If there is not a best or worst way, is it just that some ways might be better or more fun or more productive than others? Might one of the ways result in more incidental learning so that students would then be faced with less intentional learning to do later on?

The easiest way to organize the words—and seemingly the most logical way—is to group the vocabulary by kind, that is, by semantic sets. If we have 15 weeks in our semester course, this means that we could cover about 20 groups or sets of words, including presentation and practice. At that point, I would set up our 20 lessons with each lesson revolving around a vocabulary topic or semantic set. For a low-level course, we might cover semantic sets such as colors, people adjectives, family members, weather words, days of the week, months of the year, rooms in a house, kitchen words, living room words, sports, and so on.

Why semantic sets? As a teacher and a materials writer, this arrangement has always made sense. It is easy to write materials from semantic sets. Once you present the color names, you can practice using the colors in either a rote drill: "The book is *(name of color)*. I like it;" or in a communicative (two-person) drill: "What color is your *(name of object)*?" "My *(name of object)* is *(name of color)*. What color is your *(name of object)*?" This drill technique was of course widespread when the audiolingual method was in vogue, but even after this method had almost faded, the use of drills to practice semantic sets while supposedly focusing on a grammatical pattern is very much alive.

Another reason that semantic sets are popular is that it is believed (and this is the myth!) that working with the vocabulary in semantic sets actually helps learners remember the words and their meanings. Learners are told to mentally rehearse the vocabulary using the semantic sets—for example, "Apples, bananas, pears, and oranges are fruit" or "My brother's son is my nephew, and my brother's daughter is my niece." Research has shown, however, that the opposite is true. Semantic sets actually hinder and impede learning (Tinkhan 1993, 1997; Waring 1997).

Another way to organize vocabulary is by looser themes. In thematic sets of words, words that naturally occurred when discussing a given theme are included. The words are not synonyms, antonyms, coordinates, or superordinates of each other. The words have no obvious relationship to each other; their only connection is that they are all "true" with regard to the theme. For example, under the theme "planning a vacation," a learner might encounter the words *ticket, Internet, to book, a reservation, to select, a seat, an aisle seat, meal, arrival time, gate, jet,* and *silver.*

My first language course was French I in 10th grade. I recall that the textbook had a vocabulary list in each unit, and that each unit began with a dialogue telling us something about some French family. All in all, it was a fairly traditional textbook of the 1970s and '80s. (However, I imagine that textbooks today—after all of the communicative panacea in the last two decades of the last century—are still pretty much similar in many ways.)

I recall one unit in which the Martin family was going to spend their vacation in Senegal. Under this theme of "a summer vacation," we could find words such as *silver, bright, jet, first,* and *breakfast.* If the book were arranged by semantic sets, we would find a list of colors (*silver*), common descriptive adjectives (*bright*), modes of transport (*jet*), ordinal numbers (*first*), and meals (*breakfast*). Instead, we learned that the Martin family traveled from France to Senegal on a *bright silver jet.* This was their *first* time traveling to Africa. When they arrived, they were tired, but they ate *breakfast* at the hotel just after arriving. What appeared to be a random list of words was actually a list of words necessary to tell the story exemplifying the loose unit theme of a family trip.

I cannot say that this vocabulary organizational method helped me remember French vocabulary. Likewise, I cannot say that the words in the text that were grouped semantically were harder for me to remember. I was a very good student in French, and I studied hard to learn as much as I could. The question that I have now is whether I had to expend more effort to learn the words that were in semantic sets so that they would ultimately become *mine.*

Perhaps the best personal example I can give here is with the Japanese words for left *(hidari)* and right *(migi)*. I was taught both of these at the same time, but I cannot say that I learned both of them at the same time. To this day, I have a hard time remembering which is which. I have had to come up with all sorts of mnemonic devices to help me sort the two out. (It is complicated: I have to remember that *left* is shorter than *right* in English, and it is the exact opposite in Japanese, which is way too much effort to remember a direction that you need to be able to use or understand immediately.)

What the Research Says . . .

In many L2 textbooks, vocabulary is usually arranged in semantic sets. In fact, one need not look very far to find such arrangements in all proficiency levels, from low-level learners (animals: *cat, dog, monkey;* or colors: *red, blue, green*) to the most advanced learners (weather: *hail, sleet, drizzle;* or patterns: *striped, plaid, polka dot*). In most cases, there is a superordinate term with a set of member terms. In some cases, the superordinate is not explicitly stated, but the semantic set members are and the superordinate classifier is often understood.

Semantic sets are an easy way for materials writers, teachers, and curriculum designers to set up second language material. Another way to organize this material is by thematic sets. Table 6 shows an example of how the same list of 32 words could be organized in these two ways. (This is a small example; in a real example, the eights units would probably cover at least 12 words each for a total of 96 target vocabulary items.)

TABLE 6 **Two Ways of Organizing 32 Vocabulary Words**

Semantic Units	Thematic Units
Unit 1: colors	Unit 1: eating out with friends
red, blue, green, white	I like to go to this restaurant on **Saturday** nights when they serve the most **delicious fresh** shrimp **salads** you have ever eaten!
Unit 2: days of the week	Unit 2: looking at pictures of a trip
Saturday, Sunday, Monday, Tuesday	This is a picture of my **sister** and me with some friends in Greece. See. We're both in front of the **blue** and **white** Greek flag. She's the **tall** girl on my left.
Unit 3: clothing	Unit 3: going to Wimbledon
t-shirt, shoes, pants, sweater	My **brother** and I are tennis fanatics! In 2002, we went to Wimbledon! He **surfed the Internet** and found a great airfare. I loved the tennis, but I love the **strawberries** loaded with **cream** even more!
Unit 4: descriptive adjectives	Unit 4: telling a lie
long, tall, fresh, delicious	How can I tell if someone is lying? Well, I'm not very good at this, but I think the key is to look at the speaker's **eyes**. My mother is the real expert. She can find a lie so easily. She says the key is to look at the **eyelashes**—to watch how fast or slowly they move.

Unit 5: food	Unit 5: cooking something
salad, strawberries, cream, tomatoes	Today is **Tuesday**, January 7, and we're going to learn how to cook fried **green tomatoes**. This is a special dish from the South (the U.S.).
Unit 6: body parts	Unit 6: dress down Mondays
fingers, eyes, hair, eyelashes	I work in a company that has a unique dress code. Most companies now have what they call "Casual Fridays," when everyone is encouraged to dress down for a day. At my office, we have a different special clothing day: Medium Mondays. People don't like Mondays, so my boss says that is the day we should dress down. How casual can we go? Last Monday I wore a simple **t-shirt**, some khaki **pants**, and tennis **shoes**. It's called Medium **Monday** because we can't dress too casually, but we don't dress up either.
Unit 7: family members	Unit 7: a trip to the new mall
brother, sister, mother, father	I guess you could say it was a weekend shopping mania! The news report said that about 20,000 people went to the new mall on **Saturday**. Another 10,000 went on **Sunday**, so the weekend total was about 30,000 people. Can you believe these numbers? I know it's true because I was there. I guess I am now a little famous because my picture was on TV! I was easy to spot because I was wearing a bright **red sweater**.

Unit 8: hobbies	Unit 8: going on a date
play the piano, surf the Internet, listen to music, play tennis	A: "OK. I've told you about myself. Now you tell me about yourself." B: "Sure. I like to listen to music. I started **playing the piano** early. My **father** taught me when I was about 10 years old, and of course I love music. My father used to tell me that my **long fingers** would make me a natural at playing the piano, and he was right!"

There has not been a great deal of research on the use of semantic sets, but the research results are clear and, I think, very conclusive. As Table 7 shows, semantic sets are not only unhelpful, they actually hinder vocabulary retention. What our field needs is research comparing the efficacy of these two approaches with L2 students in real classes over a regular term of study (e.g., a semester). This research would include not only the obvious quantitative student learning data but also qualitative data gathered on students' impressions of their learning with each technique.

In Tinkham (1993), two experiments compared the learning rates of the same ESL learners who were learning semantically related and then semantically unrelated target vocabulary items. Results of this study showed that the learners were able to learn the semantically unrelated target items much more quickly than they could do with the semantically related items. Learners who were given words that share a common superordinate concept (such as words for colors) in list form need more time to learn these words than words that do not have a common superordinate. Thus, findings of this study strongly suggest that students have more difficulty learning new words presented to them in semantic clusters than they do learning semantically unrelated words.

TABLE 7 L2 Research on Semantic and Thematic Sets

Study	Purpose	Findings
Tinkham (1993)	To compare the learning rates of the same ESL learners who were learning semantically related and then semantically unrelated target vocabulary items	Students had more difficulty learning new words presented to them in semantic clusters than they did learning semantically unrelated words.
Waring (1997)	To replicate Tinkham's (1993) findings with Japanese speakers	Learners needed about 50% more time to learn the related word pairs than the unrelated pairs.
Tinkham (1997)	To compare the efficacy of learning words in semantic sets and in thematic sets; to compare this efficacy in oral and written modalities	Both oral and written modalities found that semantic clustering was detrimental to vocabulary learning while thematic clustering facilitated learning; however, the positive effect of thematic learning was not as strong as the negative effect of semantic clustering.
Olsen (1999)	To describe Norwegian EFL learners' errors and possible strategies in learning grammar and vocabulary	Similar vocabulary pairs *(sea-see, want-won't, lose-loose)* taught together may have caused learner errors.

Waring (1997) replicated Tinkham's 1993 study. Both studies examined the efficacy or inefficacy of presenting new vocabulary in semantic sets. However, Waring examined Japanese speakers' ability to learn artificial words in two experiments.

In Experiment 1, Japanese speakers were presented with six words paired with six imaginary words. Three of the word pairs were from a related set *(shirt, jacket, sweater)*, and three pairs were from an unrelated set *(rain, car, frog)*. Waring found that learners needed about 50 percent more time to learn the related word pairs than the unrelated pairs.

In Experiment 2, the same participants were given two sets of word pairs. The word pairs in the related words set had a common superordinate concept (fruit: *melon, apple, strawberry, grape, peach, orange*). The word pairs in the unrelated words set did not have a common semantic base (*mountain, shoe, flower, mouse, sky, television*). Again, Waring found that learners needed about 50 percent more time to learn the related word pairs than the unrelated pairs.

Waring's 1997 work is important because it replicated a previously done study, something that our field of second language acquisition has not seen enough of, and it confirmed a previous finding. This study is also valuable because the participants were Japanese speakers, thus adding more generalizability to Tinkham's 1993 findings. Finally, the use of artificial words that were so carefully constructed based on number of syllables, pronunciation, and initial and final letters allowed the researcher to control for any previous knowledge of the target words. (Since the words were original creations, it is impossible that the participants had any previous knowledge. Because of the widespread use and influence of English worldwide, it is difficult but necessary to control for this extraneous variable in studies using English words.)

Building upon these findings that semantic clustering hinders learning, Tinkham (1997) compared semantic clustering with thematic clustering, a presentation method seen more and more in language textbooks. As in Waring's study, Tinkham conducted two experiments that used artificial words; however, this study was conducted with English speakers. One experiment was conducted orally; the second was conducted with written words as in Waring (1997) and Tinkham

(1993). Both modalities produced very similar findings: *semantic clustering of new L2 vocabulary was detrimental to vocabulary learning while thematic clustering facilitated learning.* One finding of interest is that the positive effect of thematic learning was not as strong as the negative effect of semantic clustering. In other words, thematic learning is helpful to varying degrees with different learners; semantic clustering, on the other hand, proved to be detrimental in almost all cases.

One note and a related caveat on this research are necessary here. All three of these research studies used nonsense words as the target words and L1—either English (Tinkham 1993, 1997) or Japanese (Waring 1997)—for the meaning. While the use of imaginary words increased the internal validity of the experiments by allowing the researchers to control for the extraneous variable of previous knowledge of the target vocabulary items, it remains to be seen what results would be obtained with L2 students learning L2 words. Tinkham (1997) used English speakers in educational psychology classes, and none of these studies used real L2 words.

Future research must be conducted with actual L2 students and actual L2 words to confirm the experimental results. Though Olsen's (1999) descriptive study of Norwegian EFL learners focused primarily on cross-linguistic influences on learner errors, one interesting conclusion was that external factors such as teaching confusing pairs such as *sea* and *see*, *by* and *buy*, *want* and *won't*, or *lose* and *loose* at the same time actually causes errors. Olsen recommends that each word be taught in its own context at different times.

What You Can Do . . .

1. Do not present words initially in semantic sets.

The extant research is quite clear on this. Words presented in semantic sets are much harder to learn. Semantic sets would include words with a superordinate (weather: *drizzle, sleet, hail*), near synonyms (*persuade/convince, tactic/strategy, goal/aim*), and antonyms (*left/right, hot/cold, push/pull*).

2. Use thematic presentations of new words when possible.

It is certainly harder to plan thematic presentations, but research seems to indicate that this type of presentation aids retention of new vocabulary. As you choose a theme and begin your planning, try to incorporate themes that will naturally require the target vocabulary words.

3. Teach the most frequent words first; then cover other items within that semantic set.

Nation (2000) reports that the frequency ordering for the color words in English (from most common to least common) is as follows: *white, red, black, blue, green, yellow, pink, orange. Red* and *black*, for example, are 20 times more frequent than *orange*. Since learners may confuse *orange* with *yellow* or *red*, teachers should wait to present this color name until after the more common members have been learned.

Of the names of the days of the week, *Tuesday* occurs twice as often as *Thursday*. Since ESL learners often confuse these two days because they are both middle-of-the-week days and begin with T, they should not be taught at the same time. Instead, Tuesday, which occurs twice as often in real usage, should be taught first. When students know this item well, then they can be taught the competing term of Thursday.

4. Use exercises and activities that juxtapose semantic set members for reviewing items, not for initial learning.

Looking at a semantic set makes good sense when reviewing vocabulary. A worksheet activity may ask students to differentiate two or more words from the same semantic set:

1. *eggplant, cucumber, lettuce, cabbage*
2. *sweater, jacket, coat, overcoat*
3. *die, kick the bucket, pass away, cease*

Quite often words from several semantic sets are the basis for language games. Many teachers are familiar with a game such as "Jeopardy." The teacher draws a grid on the board as shown and has question cards created for each question/value:

JEOPARDY !™			
Colors	Place Names	Kitchen Things	Opposites
$100	$100	$100	$100
$200	$200	$200	$200
$300	$300	$300	$300
$400	$400	$400	$400
$500	$500	$500	$500

The questions within each category should get more difficult as the point value increases. Here are some sample questions for the category Colors:

- Colors $100: red, orange, green. Which color means "to go" on a traffic light?
- Colors $200: purple, violet, brown. Which one is most unlike the other two?
- Colors $300: gray, pink, orange. Which color is also the name of a fruit?
- Colors $400: blue, yellow, green. Which color word also means *sad*?
- Colors $500: pink, yellow, red. Which color noun is also a verb that means to change to that color?

Many teacher training coursebooks promote the use of semantic maps or distinctive feature charts. These charts focus on contrasting members of a semantic set, as in this example:

	refers to the economy	refers to money	refers to low cost	positive tone	negative tone	neutral tone
economic	X	X				X
economical		X	X	X		
cheap		X	X		X	X

This kind of activity, which uses near synonyms, would be very confusing to learners who are learning all three of these words for the first time. However, it could be an excellent tool for reviewing mostly known or at least superficially known vocabulary.

4

The use of translations to learn new vocabulary should be discouraged.

In the Real World . . .

WHEN I TAUGHT IN JAPAN, I HAD THE great opportunity to actually be a student in an intensive Japanese course for nonnative speakers. Though many ESL and foreign language teachers have studied a language in a foreign language classroom, not many of us ever have the chance to be a student for 25 hours a week. Having done both, I can say that being a student in the intensive course setting in the country where the language is spoken is a unique and rich experience.

I was in level two of a seven-level program. We had three different teachers for our five hours each day. The best teacher that I had in this program was the ideal second language teacher. She knew some English, but she would never ever speak English with us. She made us speak our broken Japanese in class, which was a good thing because the 12 students were from Brazil, China, India, Malaysia, Morocco, the Philippines, Sweden, Thailand, and the United States. She was also a good teacher for this level because she had great presentation skills for low-level students (she could speak $i + 1$ incredibly well!).

One day the teacher was trying to explain a certain grammar point. I believe it was a new verb tense. To do this, she gave the example of how when people arrive at a Japanese family's house, the family might serve something to the people. Here was my problem. I could not tell what was happening after the serving. What was the phrase that the teacher kept mentioning? I guessed that it was food, but that was all I could guess. Was this a meal? Was this a box of food? (The teacher kept talking about how nice the food looked, but in Japan, food is almost always beautifully presented.) Was this a kind of food? She kept saying it was small, but *what* was small? The plate was small? The box was small? The food was small? The amount of the food was small?

Having the patience of the perfect language teacher, the instructor explained the scenario to the class one more time. It soon became apparent that I was the only one who did not get it. The purpose of this teacher talk was to exemplify the verb tense, but I could not relate to the grammar point. I was getting nothing out of this lesson. My brain was focusing so heavily on this food or dish to which the teacher kept referring. The teacher looked at me and explained the story a third time. The rest of the class was getting a little restless, and I felt very uncomfortable because it was clear that I was the one holding up the class.

At one point, the student seated behind me, Karina from Sweden, leaned over and said in a low voice, "It's a kind of hors d'oeuvre," and with that, suddenly everything became clear. Karina had translated the unknown phrase for me. Once I was armed with this translation, the teacher repeated her story for us, and this time the whole thing made perfectly good sense to me. In fact, I was able to absorb the story and focus on the grammar point being illustrated in the story.

Translations are not bad. It is what most students do. I learned the hard way that a brief translation of a key concept at the right time can be invaluable. By *translations* (plural), I am not talking about the fairly common practice of translation in foreign language classes. Translation may or may not aid in second language vocabulary growth. In the plural sense I am referring to the use of having *translations* for the L2 target word as a source of input.

What the Research Says . . .

Perhaps the simplest of all definitions is an L1 translation. A translation gives learners instant information about the basic meaning of the L2 word. The English word book becomes *kitab* in Arabic, *hon* in Japanese, *buku* in Malay, *libro* in Spanish, and *Buch* in German. Using translations is such an obvious technique that one of the earliest methods of learning a second language depended heavily on it—that is, the Grammar-Translation Method. If translations are so good, then why do so many educators still believe the myth that learning new vocabulary with translations is a poor way to learn new vocabulary?

For some years, it was not popular to discuss the role of the learner's L1. Nagy and Herman (1987) note that studies of L1 to L2 transfer went out of vogue in the 1970s. The rise of cognitive psychology and Chomskian linguistics led to approaches in second language acquisition research that emphasized the learner's "active and creative construction." These researchers add, however, that "the existence of cross-linguistic influences is undeniable" (p. 433).

The fear exists that the L2 class is becoming an L1 class with some L2 thrown in for decoration. Teachers are afraid that if they do not actively stomp out the use of the native languages in the English class, then students will not try to speak English. This *is* true. I know that in my early teaching days, I was not sure of how to handle the use of students' L1. Early on, in fact, I often used Spanish in my ESL classes—until two non-Spanish-speaking students complained to the director! These students were right: English class is for English.

What is very different, however, is a classroom in which students translate vocabulary (or whatever the lesson is) in their heads or in their notebooks. Doing this is not intrusive. Doing this actually aids the learners in remembering these vocabulary items. These translations help.

Another argument against translations is that the use of the L1 in class can become a crutch (Rivers & Temperley, 1978). Again, teachers are responsible for maintaining an English class. This means that the class should be taught in English with a great deal of English input. In

EFL settings, however, where all of the students speak the same L1, or in some ESL settings where all of the students share a common L1, it can be helpful to translate some things. The concern expressed by Rivers and Temperley deals with overall language use in the classroom. Here we are concerned with the most effective way or ways for a given learner to acquire as much L2 vocabulary as possible in the most efficient manner. Research here is clearly on the side of translations.

Gefen (1987) claims that using the L1 encourages "lazy minds and so inhibits the transfer of the new item to long-term memory" (p. 42). Most people reading this book speak a second (or third or fourth) language. All of us translated vocabulary items. This logically occurred when we were beginners in the language, but it also continued or continues through more advanced levels. When a native speaker of Japanese uses a word that I'm not sure of, I will ask that person in Japanese, if I know him or her reasonably well, what the word means. The Japanese speaker then proceeds to explain the word to me in Japanese—sometimes with comprehensible input, sometimes not. In either case, as I'm listening to the explanation, I believe I can sense that I am thinking in Japanese (many times), but as soon as I have that "Eureka!" moment, I know that I actually translate the word "Oh, it means X!" My experience has been that this act has neither made my mind lazy nor inhibited the transfer of that word to long-term memory.

Another argument against learning new vocabulary through translations is that supposedly there are many words that do not have one-to-one translation equivalents. The question then is whether this is really true, and if it is true, to what extent is it true?

To be sure, words that seem to defy exact translations do exist. Some English words just do not seem to translate well. An example of this is our word *lap*, as in "The baby was sitting in his lap." For whatever reason, many languages do not have a word to express this concept. The English time words *afternoon* and *evening* seem to present problems as they do not mean the same thing in some languages. Sometimes one begins earlier in one language than it does in English; sometimes one ends later in one language than it does in English.

Likewise, some L2 words seem to defy translation into English or at best have only loose translations. In Malay, for example, *afternoon* and its supposed equivalent *tengahari*, *evening* and *petang*, and *night* and *malam* do not match up exactly. In Japanese, when one arrives home, one says, "*Tadaima*," to which the person in the house says, "*Okaeri nasai*." Though the latter could be translated as welcome back or welcome home, there is no equivalent English expression for the former. (One could argue that the translations are "I'm home" and "Welcome back," but these are rare occurrences in English; in Japanese, they are the norm.) A similar example is the Spanish term *buen aprovecho*, which is used just before a meal as the French use *bon apetit*. The English translation of this is silence. We do not say anything in this "slot." (We might say, "Wow, this food looks great!" to fill the sociolinguistic slot, but we do not by any stretch of the imagination regularly say, "Enjoy your meal," unless we work as a server in a restaurant.) Finally, perhaps we English speakers grew so tired of translating the French term *coup d'etat* as "a violent sudden overthrow of a government" that we just adopted *coup d'etat* to mean *coup d'etat*.

These translation attempts show that there are a few words that do not translate well. However, it is very important to note clearly that the number of these words is actually quite small. In fact, it is miniscule in the big language picture. The current misconception is that there are many words that do not have one-to-one translation equivalents—so many as to render translations a worthless vocabulary learning aid. In my 30-plus years of language experience, I have studied French, Spanish, Japanese, Malay, German, and Arabic, and this is simply not true.

Try to think of a word in a foreign language that you know that does *not* have an equivalent in English. While I am sure that you can think of some, I will bet that this list is actually quite small. I will also bet that when you have written down the tenth word, you will find yourself really scratching your head to come up with more examples. Even if you could find 100 (and this would take you a long time to do!), English has a seemingly infinite number of words. (The *American Heritage Dictionary* has about 350,000 entries; *Webster's* has about 450,000; the *Oxford English Dictionary* has more than 600,000 entries. Not included in these counts are phrasal verbs, idioms, and fixed expressions.) Therefore, it should be obvious that there are only a relatively few words that do not have a one-to-one equivalent translation in a foreign language.

Another argument against translations is that students will mistranslate the word when they look it up in their bilingual dictionary. This is not supporting evidence against translations. This is actually supporting evidence against (1) badly written dictionaries and (2) students' poor dictionary skills. Teachers tend to look down on bilingual dictionaries in general, preferring that students either guess the word from context or look it up in a monolingual (English-English) dictionary. However, using a monolingual dictionary in itself almost requires a special vocabulary. For example, an English-English dictionary might define *convince* as "persuade," and that same dictionary might ignore the fact that *come up with* is a phrasal verb and leave students with a less than satisfactory synonym of "produce, yield."

Some say that translation of a word in one language to a word in a second language does not give the learner enough knowledge to be able to use the word. No one is claiming that a learner can go from no knowledge to full productive use of the word from a single translation—but then I do not know of *any* learning technique that allows this. As was discussed in the Introduction, knowing a word involves many pieces of information about a word, and these pieces are learned in increments. Knowing a word—i.e., learning a word well enough so that it becomes part of a learner's active vocabulary—takes time and is hardly ever a "now it's off; now it's on" proposition.

Finally, one argument against the use of translations is that words are polysemous—that is, a single word can have several meanings, so how can you translate it? A good example in English is the word *state*, which has at least four different meanings. As a verb, it means "say or tell." As a noun, it can mean "condition" or "geographical area smaller than a country but bigger than a city" or "a nation" (as in Secretary of State). Another example is the word *commit*, which means "make or do." Examples of this usage are *commit suicide, commit a robbery,* or *commit a crime*. Commit also means "dedicate resources toward," as in "The company *committed* a million dollars to improving its computers." This second definition is the one that is exemplified in the passive construction "be committed to," as in "She is *committed* to the success of her new business."

Clearly, these meanings of *state* and *commit* are different. I would argue that these are in fact different words. It is time for ESL educators to stop relying on our past English-English instruction for native speakers as a basis for constructing our view of ESL, which is of course much newer than English for native speakers. The two types of instruction are enormously different. When an ESL learner is learning the word *state,* there is no reason to teach him or her all the meanings at one time. Likewise, it is not correct to say that he or she does not know the word *state* because he or she does not know all four meanings. I would argue that these four definitions are in fact for four different words (or three perhaps, since the last two are from the same concept). The two examples of *commit* are vastly different so that they should be regarded as two words.

Perhaps the best example is the word *take.* In English, *we take medicine, we take a taxi, we take a shower, we take an income tax deduction* (if we're lucky), *we take something the wrong way, we take something from one place to another,* and then *we take a break.* Try to translate these expressions into another language. You will quickly see that a different vocabulary item is needed for each usage of the English word *take.*

The example of *take* is offered to show that the problem with translating here is that for ESL purposes, what needs to be translated here is not *take* but rather *take medicine, take a taxi, take a shower,* etc., because these are idiomatic. As discussed in the Introduction, second language vocabulary learning involves more than single words. There are many kinds of "words," and these expressions prove this.

Polysemy is something that ESL learners need to grapple with early on in their language learning experience. When using translations for learning new vocabulary, learners and teachers need to remember that a word is not always a single word but rather a chunk of several words, and *that* is what needs to be translated. Thus, the problem is not translation per se but rather translation of the wrong items.

We have read a little of what opponents of translation in learning foreign language vocabulary think. This myth has maintained itself well over the years. However, current thinking in the study of L2 vocabulary makes use of translations. For example, when it comes time to test for whether a learner has learned a word, translations are certainly a viable option. One of the most widely used vocabulary measures is the Vocabulary Knowledge Scale (VKS), an instrument developed and validated by Paribakht and Wesche (1993). The VKS has five levels of "knowing a word." For each word tested, students self-report the extent of their knowledge of a word through these five levels:

1. I don't remember having seen this word before.
2. I have seen this word before, but I don't know what it means.
3. I have seen this word before, and I *think* it means

   _____.

   (provide an English synonym or an L1 translation)
4. I *know* this word. It means

   _____.

   (provide an English synonym or an L1 translation)
5. I can use this word in a sentence. Write your sentence here: _____

   (If you do #5, be sure to do #4 also.)

In order to receive a perfect mark of five points (Step 5), the learner must not only correctly use the word in a sentence but also provide an English synonym or an L1 translation (Step 4).

More and more research is showing that learning new vocabulary with translations is in fact a very good way to learn new vocabulary. Nation (1982) concluded that learning of vocabulary is faster for many learners if the meaning of the word is given through an L1 translation first. Numerous empirical studies have shown the value of L1 translations in vocabulary-learning activities (Chun & Plass, 1996; Knight, 1994; Hulstijn, 1993; Grace, 1998; Hulstijn 1992; Laufer & Hulstijn, 1998; Laufer & Shmueli, 1997; Prince, 1995).

In a study of English speakers learning French, Grace (1998) looked at the role of providing translations in computer-assisted language learning (CALL). In her rationale for conducting her study, she notes that providing the L1 translation of a word is perhaps the most controversial of all strategies and is therefore worthy of scientific study. In her study, 181 students in beginning-level first- and second-semester French classes were assigned to one of two groups: a CALL program in French with the option of English translations or a CALL program in French without an English translation. Students who had the option of verifying the translation of the language in their CALL program material scored 55 percent on an unannounced vocabulary test while those who had the same CALL program but without translations scored only 39 percent, which means that learners with access to translations acquired 42 percent more new vocabulary than those who did not. Grace therefore concludes that translation is a viable if not preferable option for many L2 learners at the beginning level. Her experiment suggests that students who had access to a glossary in L1 had a much higher retention rate of correct meanings because they had a chance to confirm the correct meanings.

In a study of 85 English-speaking students enrolled in a fourth-semester Spanish course, Jacobs, Dufon, and Hong (1994) looked at students' ability to recall material from short passages that they had read in Spanish when some students had access to L1 translations but others did not. Though this study did not look at vocabulary learning, an interesting finding in post-study questionnaires was that 99 percent of the students want glosses in their language materials. Of these students, slightly more than half preferred Spanish (L2) glosses but only if the glosses were written in Spanish that they could understand, and just under half preferred English (L1) glosses. Only an extremely small number of the students preferred Spanish (L2) glosses.

Hulstijn, Hollander, and Greidanus (1996) examined the influence of marginal glosses, dictionary usage, and reoccurrence of unknown words with 78 Dutch first-year university students of French. The researchers found that marginal gloss translations of the French vocabulary resulted in better vocabulary learning.

Teachers often say that rather than give translations, they try to draw a simple illustration of the word. One obvious problem is that some words or concepts are very difficult if not impossible to illustrate clearly, such as, *privilege, animated,* and *creamy.* What does research say about using translations and illustrations? Lotto and de Groot (1998) contrasted the use of translations versus pictures in learning foreign language vocabulary. In this study, 64 Dutch university students were presented Italian vocabulary accompanied by either a translation or a picture of the word. Word retention scores were significantly higher for the students who worked with translations than for those who had pictures.

In a study of 128 Hebrew speakers studying EFL, Laufer and Shmueli (1997) compared four modes of presentation, including lists: (1) words presented in isolation, (2) words in minimal context, i.e., in one meaningful sentence, (3) words in text context, and (4) words in elaborated text context. In each mode, half of the target words were translated into the learners' L1 and the other half were explained in English. Words glossed in L1 were always retained better than words glossed in L2. As for the context effect, words presented in lists and in sentences were remembered better than words presented in text and elaborated text. Thus, in this study, less information was better. Retention scores were higher when less information or limited context was given about the word and lower when more information or extended context was given.

Finally, Prince (1995) examined the role of the L2 proficiency of French-speaking EFL learners and whether L2 vocabulary is more effectively presented in a list of L1 translations or in a series of L2 sentences (i.e., L2 context). Prince found that less proficient students were able to recall more items when they had learned the words in the translation condition rather than in the context condition. Thus, this research showed that some students perform better when they were given only a list of L2 words and their translations.

Research is clear: *Translations are not bad but are in fact a helpful tool in learning new foreign language vocabulary.* Research should now move to more pertinent questions, such as whether the value of L1 translations is as effective for higher-proficiency students as it is for lower-proficiency students and whether certain kinds of words—e.g., concrete nouns, single-word verbs (as opposed to multiword phrasal verbs), or adjectives—lend themselves more to translation as the most effective type of initial information input.

What You Can Do . . .

1. Do not stop a student who is jotting down a translation of a new English word.

In observing ESL classes, I have seen teachers stop a student who was in the process of jotting down the L1 translation of a new English word, and say, "You need to learn to think in English." Jotting down a word or even many words in L1 will not prevent the learner from eventually being able to think in English. Translating a new word—even in your head—is a natural part of learning a word. What is unnatural is stopping or even discouraging a learner from writing down the translation in the first place.

2. Let a more knowledgeable student help another student who speaks the same language.

If you teach in a multilingual class (or even in a monolingual class), you will have some students who are better and faster at catching on to class explanations, including explanations of new vocabulary. Why not let the better students help the weaker students? I am not advocating translating out loud for everyone at the same time—primarily because this ruins the "Eureka!" moment for all of the other students. However, I encourage a better student to explain a word or two to a weaker student as long as both students are okay with this.

3. Learn what you can about your students' native language.

You do not need to be fluent in any of your students' languages. However, the more you know of the students' language, the better. (One benefit not related to vocabulary learning is that you will know when your students are talking about you!)

A little knowledge, too, can go a long way. I do not speak Portuguese or Italian. However, when I teach a class that has many speakers of Portuguese or Italian in it, I know that words such as *tolerate, cancel,* and *reconcile* will not be difficult for the students to understand. I know that these words come from Latin, and since Portuguese and Italian are Romance languages, these words should be similar. Therefore, students will recognize them as cognates as they visually translate them. I also know that the phrasal verb equivalents of these three vocabulary items—i.e., *put up with, call off,* and *make up with*—are words that are likely to be unknown and will therefore require an explanation from me and probably a mental translation from the students if not a real translation in their notebooks or books.

Guessing words from context is an excellent strategy for learning second language vocabulary.

In the Real World . . .

I REMEMBER AN EXAMPLE OF USING context clues to decipher the meaning of an unknown word when I was at the intermediate level in Spanish. At that time, I had many friends from Nicaragua who were studying at the same university where I was a student. On one occasion, I went with a small group of three or four to the supermarket to buy some ingredients that they needed to cook a special dish from Nicaragua.

I remember entering the store. I remember walking up and down the aisles rather chaotically as one of the members of our group would shout out something in Spanish and then I'd point us in the right direction to find the item. "Mantequilla," said someone, and we went to the dairy section to get the butter. "Mayonesa," said another, and we quickly went to the condiments section to get the mayonnaise.

Someone shouted, "Repollo!" I had never heard this word, but I am a good language learner and know how to use word attack skills and context clues. To me, the word was obviously composed of two parts: *re-*, which I knew meant again or very much, to a large extent, and *pollo*, which means chicken (it's where we get our English word *poultry*). We were in a supermarket shopping for food items, so the idea of pollo/chicken being the base made complete sense. The question was whether the prefix *re-* meant "again" or "to a great extent." I wondered what "chicken again" or "again chicken" could possibly mean. It did not sound promising, so I abandoned it. However, *re-* meaning "to a great extent" seemed plausible.

At that point, I headed our group toward the meat section. I led our group to just in front of the section with all of the chickens and proceeded to attempt to pick out the biggest and fattest chicken that I could since my guess was that *repollo* meant "a really, really, really big chicken."

My friends did not understand why we were in the meat section. When I explained the reason, they all laughed really hard. I didn't get it.

It turns out that *repollo* is not related to *re-* or *pollo*. The word *repollo* actually means *cabbage*.

The reason that I remember this word and its story so well is that (1) it was the only unknown word that caused a problem during that whole evening of Spanish conversation and that (2) I knew all the other words around the unknown word. Unfortunately, for most of our ESL students, conditions one and two hardly ever exist in the real world. (I also remember the word because my friends laughed at me for such a long time, but this is not something we want to encourage in class!)

What the Research Says . . .

Guessing vocabulary from context is how native speakers most frequently learn the meaning of new L1 words. There is no doubt that we were not explicitly taught all of the thousands of words that we know in our native language. The most logical explanation for this is that over the many years that we have been exposed to and interacted in our native language, we picked up these words and their meanings from context through listening and reading. To be sure, some vocabulary items were learned intentionally, but the number of such items is most likely miniscule compared to the number we have learned incidentally.

To accomplish this, we have learned to look for several clues, namely the overall topic or title, surrounding words in discourse, along with grammatical structure and intonation in speaking or punctuation in writing (Nattinger, 1988). However, it should be kept in mind that this statement refers to *native speakers learning their own native language.* Native learners are under neither the time nor task constraints that most ESL students are. Perhaps Martin (1984) says it best: "The luxury of multiple exposures to words over time and in a variety of meaningful contexts is denied to second and foreign language students. They need prodigious amounts of information within an artificially short time" (pp. 130–131). EFL learners, by virtue of not being in an English-speaking environment, have even fewer opportunities of such exposures.

The use of context clues, an integral part of reading proficiency in L1 or L2, is problematic for learning new vocabulary. Sternberg (1987) explains the situation very clearly when he says that (in L1) most vocabulary is learned from context and that this might seem to imply that teaching students to learn from context is a very effective way of increasing vocabulary growth. However—and this is an important caveat—he goes on to add that what this claim does *not* imply is that teaching specific vocabulary using context clues is the single most effective, or even a somewhat effective, way of teaching vocabulary. The idea that teaching words in context might be the best method of presentation is intuitively appealing, but Sternberg cautions that "the naturalness or typical use of a method does not imply its optimality" (p. 94). Thus, while it is possible for learners to derive vocabulary meanings from context, this procedure by itself does not foster retention of meanings (Pressley, Levin, & McDaniel 1987). In addition, Nagy and Herman (1987) state that experimental studies conducted by Margosein, Pascarella, and Pfaum in 1982 and Pressley, Levin, and

Delaney in 1982 revealed that inferring meanings from context is less effective than more intensive or explicit forms of instruction.

Numerous research studies have examined the limitations of context clues in general and in an L2 setting when vocabulary learning is the goal. Table 8 describes these studies.

TABLE 8 Context Clues Research

Study	Findings
Schatz & Baldwin (1986) English speakers	1. Native speakers were not good at guessing unknown English word meanings from real contexts. 2. Context clues in the real world are not as prevalent or useful as thought.
Hulstijn (1992) Dutch learners of French	1. When L2 learners read a passage for comprehension, they are more likely to remember the form and meaning of a word when they have inferred its meaning by themselves than when the meaning has been given to them. 2. L2 learners are more likely to infer an incorrect meaning of an unknown L2 word in an L2 text when no cue has been given to its meaning.
Wesche & Paribakht (1994) adult ESL students in the United States	1. Students in a reading-only group (reading followed by more reading) had substantial gains in word knowedge, but the gains were significantly larger in the reading-plus group (reading followed by exercises). 2. Students in the reading-plus group showed a greater depth of knowledge of the target words.

Prince (1995) French EFL learners	1. The more words you know, the more able you are to acquire new words. 2. Both lower- and higher-proficiency learners were able to learn L2 words when presented with their translations. Adding a sentence context did *not* raise learners' retention of these words.
Hulstijn, Hollander, & Greidanus (1996) Dutch EFL learners	1. When readers consult a dictionary and when the meaning of unfamiliar words has been made available through marginal glosses or when the words appear not once but three times in the text, readers usually forget the meanings immediately. 2. Learners ignore words that are not relevant for the particular reading goal. 3. Incidental vocabulary learning through reading can only explain a small percent of word knowledge.
Laufer & Shmueli (1997) Hebrew-speaking EFL learners	1. Words glossed in L1 were always retained better than words glossed in L2. 2. Words presented in lists and in sentences were remembered better than words presented in text and elaborated text. Thus, less information was better.
Nassaji (2003) adult ESL students in Canada	1. Even when learners used all stratagies available, correct guessing was low (26%). 2. Teachers should spend more time teaching vocabulary.

In a detailed study consisting of five experiments that empirically tested the hypothesis that the retention of inferred meanings is higher than the retention of given word meanings (i.e., meanings derived from context), Hulstijn (1992) reached the following conclusions: (1) When L2 learners read a passage for comprehension of content and not with the main objective of learning new vocabulary, they are more likely to remember the form and meaning of a word when they have inferred its meaning by themselves than when the meaning has been given to them; (2) L2 learners are more likely to infer an incorrect meaning of an unknown L2 word in an L2 text when no cue has been given to its meaning; and (3) the discussion in L2 methodology should not be on whether it is better to have students infer meanings instead of simply giving them the meanings, but rather the focus should be on which cue procedures are most effective—e.g., translation into L1, synonym in L2, brief sample sentence, multiple choice, or a combination of these.

At first glance, Hulstijn's first point (i.e., that learners are more likely to remember the meaning of a word if they infer the meaning by themselves) seems to be an advantage for learning in context. However—and this is a huge caveat for L2 learners—Hulstijn also found that learners are just as likely to infer a wrong meaning as the correct meaning. If an L2 learner infers the wrong meaning of a word, then that learner has to (1) receive negative feedback in some form (e.g., "I would like a *bleak* shirt, please." "*Bleak*? I'm sorry, *bleak* is not a color. Do you mean black?"); (2) understand that the communication problem is due to a lexical mistake (*bleak* vs. *black*) and not a pronunciation error; (3) figure out what the correct label in L2 is for that item (*black*); (4) discover if the mistaken word is indeed a word in L2 (yes, *bleak* is a word in the L2), what that word means (it means dark, gloomy, negative prospects), and why the learner might have confused it with the correct item (*black* means dark and *bleak* can sometimes mean dark for the sky and they have a similar form—i.e., they look alike); and (5) unlearn what he or she had inferred from context (*bleak* cannot be interchanged with *black*).

For native and nonnative speakers alike, one problem with learning words in context is that in the real world, context is often not very clear in terms of revealing the meaning of the word if the reader really does not know the word. Schatz and Baldwin (1986) found that high schools students, who were all native speakers of English, were not very successful at guessing word meanings from real contexts. In this study, half of the students worked with English sentences from actual published sources (e.g., newspapers, magazines). Each sentence contained a target word that the students did not know. The target word was a real English word, and the context was a natural context. The target word was underlined, and the sentence was followed by five words, one of which was a suitable synonym for the target word in this context. The other half of the students saw only the underlined target item and the five words. The researchers used a large sample (n = 224), but they found no significant difference between the group that had access to an actual context for the words and the group that merely guessed randomly at the meanings of the words.

If the use of context clues is problematic for native speakers, it is of course much more so for nonnative speakers. In addition to the problem of lack of vocabulary knowledge that then leads to a very limited context from which to pull context clues, L2 learners find some context clues more difficult than others. Haynes and Baker (1993) note this difficulty difference between two types of context clues. Local context clues are clues that are very near the unknown word—for example, an unknown adjective just in front of a known noun, a situation in which it is syntactically clear that the first word, whatever it may mean, is limited in meaning by the second word. On the other hand, global context clues are clues that are not located near the unknown word and for which the connections to the unknown word are not as obvious syntactically and therefore semantically. They found that L2 learners of different language groups were all rather good at using local context clues but that a high percentage of L2 learners were not able to use global context clues to ascertain basic information regarding a short reading passage. In other words, L2 learners find it difficult to integrate longer sections of a text to guess a word's meaning even when that word appears several times.

Finally, research by Prince (1995) is worth discussing here again since it directly compared learning vocabulary from translation-pair lists versus vocabulary in context. In this study, French EFL learners worked with 22 concrete nouns as target words. There were two groups of learners: weaker proficiency and stronger proficiency. In addition, there were two learning conditions: words presented in a translation-pair list and words presented in a simple L2 context (i.e., students had to figure out the correct meaning of the L2 words by themselves). There were two testing conditions for all students: a translation recall in which students had to translate a word and a context recall in which students had to fill in the blanks with the correct target word. In the translation recall, 11 words were English and required a French translation and 11 words were French and required an English translation.

Results showed that the proficiency level of the learner influenced vocabulary learning. The more advanced students had a higher rate of correct answers than did the weaker group (67 vs. 49 percent). Both groups performed statistically significantly better in the translation learning condition than in the context learning condition. The condition of recall was well within the prescribed limits of statistical significance ($p<.0001$). Learners found it easier to recall words in a translation condition than in the context condition (64 vs. 51 percent). Recall results were better in the L2–L1 direction than in the L1–L2 direction for the weaker students. (However, this direction factor was not statistically significant for either group of learners regardless of the learning condition or the recall condition.)

The most important finding of this research in terms of this current study is that L2 words were more successfully learned when presented with their translations. Adding a sentence context did not raise learners' retention of these words.

In a study of Hebrew speakers studying EFL, Laufer and Shmueli (1997) compared four modes of presentation, including lists: (1) words presented in isolation, (2) words in minimal context (i.e., in one meaningful sentence), (3) words in text context, and (4) words in elaborated text context. Mode 1 was a listing of the word and its Hebrew translation or an English synonym. Modes 2, 3, and 4 had three levels of context. Mode 2 was minimal context, mode 3 was in a brief text, and mode 4 was an elaborated text. In each mode, half of the target words were translated into the learners' L1 and the other half were explained in English. Words glossed in L1 were always retained better than words glossed in L2. As for the context effect, words presented in lists and in sentences were remembered better than words presented in text and elaborated text. Thus, in this study, less information was better. Retention scores were higher when less information or limited context was given about the word and lower when more information or extended context was given.

One explanation for this is that learners remember most easily what they notice the most easily. If a word is buried in a long context and the word itself does not stand out (by being unique looking—e.g., *xylophone* or *eggnog*—or by being repeated several times), then learners are less likely to pay attention to it. Learning can occur with noticing but not without it. Longer contexts do not promote noticing.

Reading passages as conduits to vocabulary acquisition are problematic. Maiguashca (1984) states that the reading of texts presents three methodological drawbacks from the point of view of vocabulary. First, the text is the main focus and the vocabulary is incidental. Second, the study of texts is often pedagogically uneconomical. It is inevitable that texts contain words and expressions that the teacher does not deem expedient to teach or explain at that time and texts do not always contain items that the teacher would like to include. Dealing with texts can be extremely time consuming. Finally, learning of words is only partial and passive. A key factor here may be the passive aspect. A pedagogical premise for teaching vocabulary has been that it is desirable to involve the learner actively in the *noticing, practicing,* and ultimately *learning* of an unfamiliar word. As has been pointed out, new words encountered in reading passages are frequently not dealt or interacted with by the learner.

Hulstijn, Hollander, and Greidanus (1996) note that it is a generally accepted principle that extensive L2 reading is good for vocabulary growth and that it would appear at first glance that vocabulary growth stems largely from reading and listening. On closer inspection, it turns out that learners often fail to learn the meaning of an unknown word in a text. This could be because learners simply fail to notice the new word or that learners notice the new word but choose to ignore it. Sometimes the contextual information surrounding the word is so redundant that the reader can understand the meaning of that part of the passage without knowing the exact meaning of the unknown word. Thus, the reader does not pay attention to the word. For learning to take place, "attention must be focused not exclusively on the meaning of the target word, but also on the connection between the word's form and its meaning" (p. 1).

In this study, the three researchers found that even when readers consult a dictionary and even when the meaning of unfamiliar words has been made available through marginal glosses, or even when such words appear not once but three times in the text, readers usually forget the meanings immediately. This finding suggests that incidental vocabulary learning through reading can only explain a small percent of word knowledge. Learners tend to ignore words that are not relevant for the particular reading goal. Incidental learning is not adequate; learners must engage in additional activities, namely paying attention to words deemed to be important, marking down new words, or reviewing new vocabulary regularly. Here is where practice exercises can be helpful in increasing L2 vocabulary retention.

In a study of adult intermediate ESL students in a university (n = 38), Wesche and Paribakht (1994) compared a reading-only group with a reading-plus group. The first group read four texts on two themes and answered comprehension questions. This was followed by a supplementary text especially composed to present another time the target words from the first four readings. The reading-plus group also read the same four texts and did the same comprehension questions. However, instead of doing a further reading with incidental exposure to the target words, the students in this group did vocabulary exercises focusing on the target words. Thus, both groups interacted with the target words an equal number of times.

Test results on vocabulary acquisition showed that while the reading-only group did have substantial gains in word knowledge, the gains were significantly larger in the reading-plus group. In addition, students in the second group showed a greater depth of knowledge of the target words. Because students in the reading-only group were not forced to pay attention to the word forms and/or their meanings, their lower vocabulary acquisition is not surprising.

Commenting on vocabulary teaching in L1, Chall (1987) asserts that the long-held preference for teaching words through context rather than direct teaching is based on preferences for a more natural approach to learning and teaching and on resistance to structure and system on the assumption that "natural" is better for learning. She does not, however, make a case for one over the other but rather for both. She notes that there is research showing that both direct and indirect teaching methods are effective. Students need to learn words through reading, and they need to learn words directly, apart from the context.

Reading is a very interactive process, and interactive theorists argue that guessing from context actually requires a vast vocabulary (Pino-Silva, 1993). Thus, it is the good readers—ironically—who use context clues to guess the least because they do not have to. They already know the vocabulary. Because the learning task is so great, it is unlikely that the size of vocabulary needed to read efficiently in English can be acquired by word attack skills or context clues. Therefore, direct acquisition of a great number of lexical items is imperative, especially in the early stages of learning when learners' nascent vocabulary inventory is severely limited, a belief espoused by others (Nation, 1993).

Because of their limited vocabulary knowledge, L2 readers will always be at a disadvantage and must therefore make use of context clues to the extent possible to infer the meaning of the numerous unknown words they will encounter. Unfortunately, it is exactly the L2 readers' very limited vocabulary knowledge that hinders their being able to make full use of context clues as well. In other words, compared to L1 readers, L2 readers' lack of vocabulary knowledge forces them to guess about word meanings much more often; however, this lack of vocabulary knowledge also severely limits L2 readers' ability to make use of the remaining context as context clues for guessing.

Knowing many words not only allows the reader to be able to comprehend previously learned words but also arms the reader with a larger context for when the reader is forced to use context (clues) to guess an unknown word. In other words, the greater the number of unknown words in a passage, the less context the reader has to work with to figure out the meaning of the unknown words.

In a case study at an intensive academic program in the United States (Folse, 2002), I examined how an advanced Japanese-speaking ESL student navigated through a reading assignment when he was told to use context clues, not his dictionary, upon encountering any unknown words. Using a think-aloud protocol, the student demonstrated a good knowledge of and practical skills in using context clues; however, the sheer number of unknown vocabulary items as well as lack of clear and adequate clues (Haynes & Baker, 1993; Laufer, 1997; Schatz & Baldwin, 1986) were just too much for this student to overcome. His ability to use context clues was of little use here, although technically he applied the skill of using context clues well.

To use context clues effectively, a learner has to have a large vocabulary already. Those who know more words are more likely to be able to use those known words successfully to learn even more words from context. Stanovich (1986) and James (1996) discuss the so-called "Matthew effect," the phenomenon by which the rich get richer and the poor get poorer. (The parable from which this is taken appears in Matt. 25:14–30, specifically verse 29.)

No discussion of context clues would be complete without talking about the distinction between using context clues to guess the meaning of an unfamiliar word and using context clues to learn and remember the meaning of a new word. There is support for the former but not the latter. In other words, the true pedagogical value of guessing may be for reading comprehension and not for vocabulary learning. What may be important for ultimate learning is not whether the reader guessed at the meaning or asked a native speaker but rather the role of that word in understanding part of the reading passage. If the word is deemed important for the reading task, then the learner is more likely to notice the word, and noticing greatly increases the likelihood of acquisition.

What You Can Do . . .

1. Teach the use of context clues as a good *reading* strategy, but recognize that learners cannot rely on this compensatory strategy for vocabulary growth.

The use of context clues is without a doubt a good strategy to improve reading in L1 and L2, but *it is a reading-improvement strategy, not a vocabulary-improvement strategy.* When readers encounter a new word or a piece of information that they do not understand (and not necessarily just because of vocabulary), they use their interactive reading skills to figure out the message. These skills include making predictions, using context clues, forming conclusions, and locating specific information. Any or all of them could contribute to vocabulary growth, but that is not the purpose of any of them.

Teachers should continue to teach a variety of context clues. It is important to teach the use of context clues at the phrase level (e.g., collocations), the sentence level, and the paragraph level. ESL learners are good at local context clues (i.e., those that are very near the unknown word) but not so good at global clues (i.e., those that are often located near but not next to the unknown word) (Haynes, 1993). In *Intermediate Reading Practices, 3rd edition* (Folse, 2004c), each lesson focuses on a specific context clue—namely, opposites, descriptions, cause/effect, purpose, *too/enough,* appositives, and combination of skills. It is important for you to teach your students how these and other context clue types function when the clues are near the unknown word as well as when they are not so near the target word.

It is true that context clues are not so efficient in rapidly improving learners' vocabulary, but practicing the use of context clues can improve learners' overall language ability as well as their reading ability. Since reading can result in improved vocabulary knowledge, then anything that improves reading is a good thing.

2. Choose context clues exercises and activities that match the proficiency level of your students.

Teachers also need to remember that students need to know a great deal of vocabulary in order to effectively use context clues for any unknown words. Asking students to guess words from a context that contains too many unknown words is frustrating and disheartening. Students already know that they do not know enough vocabulary; do not exacerbate the problem.

3. Exercises that ask students to guess word meanings from context should be done in class so that the teacher can give immediate feedback. Another option is to have your students do these exercises on a computer-based program that gives immediate feedback.

The rationale for having students guess word meanings from context is that the mental effort involved causes learners to remember that word and meaning better. This is in fact true. The problem is that ESL learners are just as likely to guess a wrong meaning as a right meaning, and the student will remember whatever meaning was guessed—regardless of its accuracy. Thus, the best learning situation is one in which the learners complete the context clues activity and then receive immediate feedback so that learners are not faced with incorrect guesses.

4. Reading can be a conduit for vocabulary growth, especially when done with vocabulary exercises.

In class and for homework, give your students exercises and activities that focus on vocabulary. Reading can result in vocabulary improvement, but the studies cited in this section of the book have consistently shown that more vocabulary improvement occurred when students did exercises or activities that focused student attention on the words. In other words, explicit practice was highly beneficial. Students learned not only more words (breadth) but also deeper knowledge of those words (depth).

MYTH 6

The best vocabulary learners make use of one or two really good specific vocabulary learning strategies.

In the Real World . . .

IN 1984, I WAS 24 YEARS OLD AND HAD an MA in TESOL with four years ESL teaching experience. In July of that year, I took my first EFL/overseas teaching position when I moved from Mobile, Alabama, to Riyadh, Saudi Arabia.

The teaching was tough. We had to be at school at 5 A.M. six days a week. The curriculum was based on the Defense Language Institute materials, which at that time were very formulaic and rather dry. (Shortly after my time in Saudi Arabia, the Defense Language Institute materials were extensively revised.) The plus was that our classes were rather small, with rarely more than ten students per group.

I remember an important incident that occurred within my first month of teaching there. My Saudi students were always very interested in vocabulary and would frequently stop class to ask about the meaning of an unfamiliar word. On this particular day, a student's hand went up with a vocabulary question.

He asked, "Folse, what means encyclobedia? Encyclobedia—same same dictionary?" which was how my Saudi students asked if encyclopedia meant the same as dictionary. (Arabic speakers frequently confuse /b/ and /p/, the latter being a phoneme that does not naturally exist in Arabic.)

I had taught Saudi students in my previous jobs in the United States. I knew a little Arabic. I knew that Saudi students were not only inquisitive about vocabulary but actually welcomed lists of words in class.

Even though the student had asked me for a short answer as to whether an encyclopedia was the same as a dictionary, I knew that the class could handle a better explanation than just a near synonym, and I believed that this information was important.

I proceeded, "Well, no, not exactly. You see an encyclopedia is not one book. It's actually a whole set or group of books. There is usually one book for each letter of the alphabet. Some letters are combined into one book, so the letter R has its own book while the letters V and W have one book for both letters. A dictionary is just one book, and it has about three or four lines for each word. It has the meaning of the word and its pronunciation, and sometimes it has some additional information. An encyclopedia has information about each word, but it has a lot of information, not just the meaning and spelling." I may have continued on for another minute or two as I slowly explained all of this in perfect "low-level" English.

When I had finished, the students turned to each other and conferred loudly in Arabic for about 30 seconds as I waited at the blackboard. When they had finished discussing this matter, the student who had asked the question looked straight at me and said, "OK. I see. Same same dictionary."

I tried not to show the disappointment that I felt. Obviously, this student was not a very good language learner. He did not have good vocabulary learning strategies. He was content to seek a rather superficial near synonym instead of going for a more detailed understanding of the word *encyclopedia*.

About two weeks later, I saw for the first time a copy of the standardized test on the book that my students and I had just completed. I was surprised to see that about a third of the questions in the listening section, the grammar section, and the reading section and all of the questions in the vocabulary section depended on knowledge of discrete vocabulary items. The question format was quite simple: a single word followed by four choices.

In my brief perusal of the test, I did not see a question about *encyclopedia*. However, based on the questions that I did see, if a question for *encyclopedia* had been included, I'm sure it would have looked like this:

      6. **encyclopedia**   a. animal   b. green c. dictionary d. shoes

In other words, the student who asked, "Same same dictionary?" *did* have a good strategy. Knowing a word is almost never a one-step process, so asking for a synonym or a related word may be a good first step to help learners be able to acquire the word. What is certain is that the student knew much better than I did what the standardized exam looked like. I was the new guy, not him.

What I learned in this experience was to listen to my students better. Having a master's degree in TESOL and some teaching experience did not make me an expert at the best strategies to study English in that particular course. My students knew that the standardized exit exam for that course tended to ask many simplistic vocabulary questions, so knowing synonyms for the vocabulary in the book was important to them.

What the Research Says . . .

In a nutshell, the myth of the existence of one specific magical strategy for foreign language vocabulary is false. The truth is that there are numerous good vocabulary learning strategies (VLSs), and there are bad ones, too. What research has shown us is that good learners use a wide variety of VLSs; however, the good students have developed an individualized set of strategies that works best for their needs and personalities.

Language Learning Strategies

Research regarding L2 learner general strategies seemed to peak around 1990 (O'Malley & Chamot, 1993; Wenden & Rubin, 1987). According to Oxford (1990), who developed the Strategies Inventory for Language Learning (SILL), the most influential work in language learning strategies, learning strategies are steps taken by students to enhance their own learning. Gu (2003) defines this term in more detail: "A learning strategy is a series of actions a learner takes to facilitate the completion of a learning task. A strategy starts when the learner analyzes the task, the situation, and what is available in his/her own repertoire. The learner then goes on to select, deploy, monitor, and evaluate the effectiveness of this action, and decides if s/he needs to revise the plan and action" (p. 2). Oxford (1992/93) further explains that the appropriate use of language learning strategies, which include dozens or even hundreds of possible behaviors, results in improved L2 proficiency overall or in specific skill areas (such as vocabulary).

It is also important to identify the purpose of a given strategy—for example, to understand a statement, to learn a new word, or to review previously encountered words. To be sure, strategies for learning a new word are not the same as those for reviewing a list of already encountered words. Likewise, a coping strategy for understanding a word in a reading passage, such as guessing from context, is not necessarily a good strategy for learning words. This is not to discourage or malign guessing from context as a language coping strategy; however, it is not a particularly effective vocabulary *learning* strategy. (See Myth 5 for information on the limitations of the use of context clues for vocabulary learning.)

Why should teachers care about learning strategies? To be sure, a better understanding could help us understand our students better, but there is a potentially bigger payoff. The main benefit to teachers is that these strategies can be taught to any second language learner and thus modify the learner's progress (Bialystok, 1981). Appropriate language learning strategies can result in improved proficiency and greater self-confidence.

Sometimes teaching strategies actually make learners aware of strategies that they already possess but do not use effectively or often enough. Thus, a role of learning strategies is to make explicit what otherwise may occur without the learner's awareness or may occur inefficiently during early stages of learning (O'Malley & Chamot, 1993). An application of this to vocabulary learning strategies (Pressley & Ahmad, 1986) is that of learners who had mnemonic strategies but failed to recognize their applicability. In their research, Pressley and Ahmad noted that when students were shown a simple learning strategy for memorizing the order of a set of words, they were able to apply this to their own learning, potentially resulting in better vocabulary learning. In other words, this may not entail teaching something totally new as much as it may be raising learners' consciousness of the value of certain strategies in order to increase their frequency of use.

Jones (1995) notes that learner strategies have become recognized as a prime ingredient in language learning success. The general consensus seems to be that successful learners have a wide range of strategies from which they can pull. Thus, if it is agreed that these strategies are teachable, then it logically follows that teaching learners a wide variety of strategies and their subsequent applications will enhance second language learning success, especially for less effective learners (Wenden 1986). According to Rubin (1975), what is happening inside the good language learner's head (i.e., by examining what strategies and cognitive processes are used to learn a language) may lead us to well-developed theories of the language acquisition process that can be taught to others. "The inclusion of knowledge about the good language learner in our classroom instructional strategies will lessen the difference between the good learner and the poorer one" (p. 50).

Vocabulary Learning Strategies (VLSs)

We have seen information explaining why acquiring as much vocabulary as possible is certainly important. If it is accepted that acquisition of more vocabulary is our goal but that there are simply too many words in the language for all or most of them to be dealt with one at a time through vocabulary instruction, then what is the next logical step?

Commenting primarily on reading issues, Nagy and Herman (1987) conclude that there are better ways to spend the considerable time that would be required for extensive word-by-word vocabulary instruction, such as free reading or learning comprehension strategies. Carter and McCarthy (1988) add that "it is impossible to teach learners all the words they need to know, and so it is important to teach them guessing strategies that will enable them to tackle unknown words and lose their reliance on dictionaries. This is the beginning of viewing vocabulary learning as a language skill, or shifting the responsibility to the learner" (p. 42).

Taking a middle-of-the-road position, Graves (1987) concludes that though some of the words that students need to learn should be taught directly, students additionally need to develop strategies for learning words by themselves as well as an attitude that will encourage the continued use of these strategies. "Regardless of how much instruction we do in schools, students will actually do most of their learning independently. It therefore makes sense to encourage students to adopt personal plans to expand their vocabularies over time" (p. 177). Sternberg (1987) concurs that it is critical in teaching vocabulary to train students to teach themselves because no matter how many words we teach students directly, this will be only a fraction of what they will be required to know. Thus, one of the main classroom activities for teachers of vocabulary is the direct teaching of learning strategies related to vocabulary.

Research has identified numerous vocabulary learning strategies. Research has also looked at how these strategies are used, which students use them, and whether training students in strategy use results in more vocabulary learning.

One of the most important studies on VLSs was done by Sanaoui (1995). Teachers always want to know what the one best VLS is; the answer is that it does not exist. There is not one single VLS that works for everyone. In a case study of French learners in British Columbia, Sanaoui (1995) found two distinct approaches among learners with regard to learning vocabulary: structured and unstructured. Learners' proficiency level and type of instruction did not impact their vocabulary learning; what mattered was *the individual learner's approach* toward overall vocabulary learning: structured or unstructured. While Sanaoui (1995) did not find one "best" strategy from learners in her study, she did find that the good learners had a definite plan or strategy for learning English, including vocabulary, while the weaker students did not. In other words, it does not seem to matter so much *what* students do with new vocabulary *provided that they do something and that they do it consistently*. Thus, students should write a translation, think of an original sentence in their head, or repeat the word five times—whatever works for them. However, regardless of which strategy or strategies they focus on, they should do this consistently.

Learners using a structured approach engaged in independent study, initiated learning activities and opportunities, recorded the lexical items being learned, reviewed vocabulary notes, and practiced the vocabulary outside of class; those using an unstructured approach either did not do these things or did not do them consistently or to the same degree. Sanaoui (1996) makes a solid case for teaching VLSs, concluding that course time be spent on helping students become autonomous learners who are able to strengthen their vocabularies on their own, both in and outside classrooms.

In one of the earliest studies of VLSs with one particular group of learners, Ahmed (1989) surveyed 300 Sudanese EFL learners. In this study, the good learners used VLSs more than the poor learners did. In addition to overall use, the good learners used a wider variety of VLSs. Subsequent research with other nationalities and languages confirmed these results.

O'Malley, Chamot, Stewner-Manzanares, Kupper, and Russo's 1985 study (as cited in O'Malley & Chamot, 1993) investigated whether strategy instruction in a natural classroom setting would result in improved learning on speaking, listening, and vocabulary tasks. The students were divided into three groups: metacognitive strategies, cognitive strategies, and control. Though a basic result was that the students in the metacognitive and cognitive groups used the strategies in which they had been trained, there were no significant differences overall among the treatment groups for the vocabulary tasks. When the results were analyzed by ethnic group, however, it was found that the Asian control group outperformed the Asian training groups and that the Hispanic training groups outperformed the Hispanic control groups. The teachers in the study indicated that the Asians preferred to use rote memorization, which is what the control group was using, while the Hispanic students had shown more interest in the alternatives to their usual learning strategies. In another study, Politzer and McGroarty (1985) found that the cultural background of the students had a great deal to do with the type of language learning behavior likely to be used by students.

In a study of English speakers learning Hebrew as a second language, Cohen and Aphek (1981) sought to examine ways that second language learners could make their own overall task as easy as possible. The researchers focused on vocabulary learning strategies and examined what kinds of word associations second language learners made. They found that even though only 13 students reported that they made use of associations, they reported incorporating as many as 11 different types of associations. Cohen and Aphek (1978) found that only one of the vocabulary learning strategies correlated with vocabulary learning, namely coining a term. For example, learners might create a compound from the simpler lexical items (e.g., a learner not knowing *balloon* in Hebrew used simpler known Hebrew words to represent "air ball"). The frequent coining of terms correlated significantly with the vocabulary learning task, suggesting that this strategy makes for good vocabulary learning.

Hulstijn, Hollander, and Greidanus (1996) conducted a study of Dutch-speaking advanced students of French who had to read a passage and then answer questions about vocabulary from the passage. The researchers concluded that learners failed to notice the presence of unfamiliar words in reading and listening contexts. Furthermore, even if they do notice unfamiliar terms, they may simply decide to ignore or avoid them in reading and listening. Incidental learning is not adequate; learners must engage in additional activities, namely paying attention to words deemed to be important, marking down new words, or reviewing new vocabulary regularly.

Lessard-Clouston (1994) conducted a study that was designed to challenge students to reflect on what they do in order to learn English words by answering questions about their vocabulary learning strategies. VLSs associated with a structured approach such as keeping written records and reviewing words were identified. Lessard-Clouston had students discuss VLSs in class, and students who did not follow a structured approach were able to see that contrast between their own VLSs and those thought to facilitate learning more vocabulary.

In researching his own study of Hungarian, Jones (1995) identified three specific strategies that proved helpful to him. These were auditory rehearsal, keyword imagery, and target-language etymology. Because Hungarian is so far removed from other European languages, English cognates and other lexical similarities are rare, thus allowing for a close focus on lexical acquisition strategies and processes without L1 interference.

Because of the limited role of vocabulary teaching over the years, there have been only a small number of what could be called distinct "methods" for teaching vocabulary. By far, the best known of these methods is the **keyword method**, which is a VLS involving imagery as well as the L1 in learning the L2.

The keyword method is a two-stage process that uses mnemonic devices and interactive imagery to facilitate vocabulary acquisition in L2. In the first stage, learners form their own acoustic association between the target word and any word in L1. In the second stage, learners form an image link between the target L2 word and the L1. For example, to learn the Japanese word for *chair* 'isu,' an English-speaking learner would first try to commit the pair *isu = chair* to memory while thinking of the phrase "it is easy (sounds like *isu*) to sit in a chair."

Ott, Butler, Blake, and Ball (1973) found that experimental groups using interactive-image mnemonics remembered twice as many words as control groups did. Data from self-reports suggested that over 75 percent of the words that were remembered by students across all treatment conditions, including the control groups, were learned by these elaborative strategies. The results suggest that the use of elaborative devices, either spontaneously or by design, is a natural and effective way for students to approach the learning of new vocabulary.

Kaspar (1993) not only touts this method but also provides pertinent information for implementing this procedure in class. She notes that research on this method has shown that if words are taught in blocks of three and then immediately tested (i.e., learners attempt to retrieve what they have learned), recall levels reach near 100 percent.

Sternberg (1987) has criticized the keyword method because it requires a great deal of mental effort, something that learners may not be willing to do in the long run. He compares it to speed reading in that, while it may be efficient, it is taxing and therefore likely to be abandoned. However, no research has been presented to back this up. What is factual is that the keyword method works. What is more impressive is that it appears to work for very long-term retention.

A more commonly cited concern with this "quick learning" approach is that the recall levels might not be so impressive later on. Beaton, Gruneberg, and Ellis (1995), however, found that this was not the case. Their case study of a learner who had studied Italian using a keyword method ten years earlier showed that the individual was able to recognize slightly more than half of the items on an initial vocabulary test and that after spending only ten minutes looking at a vocabulary list, the individual's recall level rose dramatically. The authors make a distinction between vocabulary storage and vocabulary retrieval. With appropriate cues (here, the learner reviewed a vocabulary list for ten minutes), access can be made to knowledge that has been retained but not necessarily recalled.

Pressley, Levin, Kuiper, Bryant, and Michener (1982) identified the keyword/definition linkage as critical to enhanced recall of definitions from vocabulary items. In their study, control students worked with definitions only while treatment groups used imagery (i.e., the keyword method). The authors found that increased semantic processing of definitions does not strengthen the mental linkages between a vocabulary word and its definition but that encoding meaningful interactions between a keyword and the definition does strengthen the association. In other words, the act of thinking about the word and its definition was not as helpful in remembering a word as was thinking about a visual association of an L1 keyword with the L2 word.

In a study of Arabic-speaking EFL learners, Brown and Perry (1991) examined the results of three groups of students who used a keyword method, a semantic method, and a combination keyword-semantic method. The study produced evidence that the keyword method in combination with semantic processing was more effective than either of the two approaches alone. These findings are consistent with predictions made by depth-of-processing theory (Craik & Lockhart, 1972; Craik & Tulving, 1975; Schouten-van Parreren, 1995) that the more learners have to engage their brain when learning a word, the more likely they will be to acquire the word.

Although Brown and Perry (1991) found good results for the keyword method combined with semantic processing, the researchers note three potential shortcomings of the keyword method. First, this method has been used more successfully with individual learners than with classes of students, an important factor since most vocabulary learning in the classroom occurs in group presentation. The authors' second caveat, that the superiority of keyword method over a no-strategy situation decreases over time, was refuted in several studies, including the previously cited study by Beaton, Gruneberg, and Ellis (1995). Last, the effectiveness of the keyword method, at least with native speakers, seems to be connected to the verbal ability of the student—that is, an individual learner variable. Perhaps this particular kind of method would not be suitable for classroom use as it may not help a whole sector of the class.

Using imagery is an important strategy, but there are many others. Schmitt and Schmitt (1993) sought to produce a list of vocabulary learner strategies and then to quantify the use of these strategies. They first carried out a small project to compile a basic list of vocabulary learning strategies. They consulted textbooks for strategies, they asked intermediate Japanese students about their own strategies, and they asked the teachers to add other possible strategies to the list. The strategies were then divided into two classes: (1) initial learning of a new word's meaning and (2) studying and remembering the word's meaning once it is known (i.e., practicing). The list was further subdivided into six areas under initial learning of a meaning and ten areas under studying and remembering the meaning. In the final phase of the study, 600 Japanese EFL students were asked to survey the complete list of 36 strategies to indicate which of the strategies they employed as well as whether they thought the particular strategy was helpful. Students were also asked to rate the five most helpful strategies.

Using a questionnaire adapted from Sanaoui's dissertation, Kojic-Sabo and Lightbown (1999) surveyed 47 ESL and 43 EFL students to identify the strategies the learners used in learning English vocabulary. Although there were individual differences among the 90 students, most fell into one of eight profiles of set strategies. The researchers found that students with higher levels of achievement had more frequent and elaborate strategy use. In addition, the researchers concluded that time and learner independence were the two factors most associated with success in vocabulary learning and higher overall English proficiency. In other words, the more successful vocabulary learners were those who spent more time on task—by studying, initiating opportunities for practicing vocabulary, and being exposed to the target items—and who were able to learn independently, which is part of what Sanaoui (1995) called a "structured approach" to vocabulary learning.

One of the most commonly taught ESL classes at the higher-proficiency level is a TOEFL® preparation class, and vocabulary certainly plays a big role in that class. In a case study of 14 ESL learners in his own class, Lessard-Clouston (1996b) found that students did not approach vocabulary learning in a structured way. This is quite surprising since vocabulary is so important on the TOEFL®, and students are certainly well aware of this.

Rasekh and Ranjbary (2003) studied the effect of metacognitive strategy training on 53 Iranian EFL college-age students in two classes. In their regular English course consisting of ten weeks (four hours a day, three days a week, total of 120 instruction hours), the two classes of students were randomly assigned to a control group and experimental group. Both classes used the same textbook, which emphasized the role of lexical knowledge in learning English, and both classes were taught by the same instructor, one of the researchers. The groups were tested initially for vocabulary knowledge and overall English proficiency; no statistically significant differences were found.

The sole difference between the two groups was that the experimental group received explicit instruction in metacognitive strategies beginning from the second day of the course. Throughout the ten weeks, the students in the experimental group were reminded of strategy use; appropriate strategies for various words were discussed. A vocabulary post-test at the end of the course showed that the experimental group had higher vocabulary scores. Since the groups were initially equivalent, used the same course materials, met for the same length of time, and had the same instructor, any difference in vocabulary gain could reasonably be attributed to the sole differentiating factor, namely metacognitive strategy training.

As Rasekh and Ranjbany (2003) state, "In other words, the explicit instruction and practice the experimental group received about how to plan their vocabulary learning, set specific goals within a time frame, select the most appropriate vocabulary learning strategy, monitor strategy use, use a combination of strategies, self-testing degree of mastery of the new vocabulary items after meeting the words for the first time, managing their time by devoting some time during their study hours to vocabulary practice, and finally evaluating the whole process, contributed to this improved and expanded lexical knowledge" (p. 12).

The researchers' conclusion then is that both learners and teachers must become aware of learning styles and strategies through strategy instruction. They also note that EFL learners—who are by virtue of their learning environment not exposed to a great deal of English input that would allow greater incidental learning—must receive more and better strategy training. In addition, EFL textbook writers need to dedicate more space to strategy training.

Many studies have looked at how learners use dictionaries. (See Myth 7 for more on this.) Beech (1997) found that young Greek EFL learners did not translate target words adequately due to poor dictionary use skills, a strategy in which learners could certainly be trained. Laufer and Hill (2000) studied what lexical information L2 learners select in a CALL dictionary and the effect of this lookup behavior on vocabulary learning. Interesting work (Laufer & Hadar, 1997) has also been done on the interaction between students' proficiency and strategies when looking up words in different kinds of dictionaries, namely monolingual, bilingual, and bilingualized dictionaries. (Bilingualized dictionaries have entries in the target language with explanations in the native language along with examples in the target language. For some educators and some students, this is the ideal compromise.)

In a large EFL program, Kudo (1999) described and systematically categorized vocabulary-learning strategies of Japanese high school students. In the two parts of this study, 325 and then 504 Japanese senior high school students completed a questionnaire about the frequency of 56 VLSs. Descriptive statistics indicated that many strategies were infrequently used. Two results matched those found in earlier research. First, cognitively demanding strategies such as the keyword method were not common while less demanding VLSs such as verbal repetition were frequent. Second, the categories that resulted from cluster analysis were consistent with Oxford's (1990) classification based on her research conducted in the United States.

Gu and Leung (2002) examined English errors made by 60 Chinese and 65 Hong Kong EFL non-English majors. The researchers sought to identify student strategies that may have accounted for the errors. The researchers found evidence that the way the learners were taught English early on as well as the L1 influenced the types of learner errors. Chinese learners often produced mistranslations that seemed illogical in English, such as mixing up the word *precious* for *cherish* or *expensive,* because the three words share a Chinese character that is not obvious in English.

In a very large study of 1,067 EFL learners at institutions of higher learning, Fan (2003) looked at Hong Kong learners and VLSs. In particular, Fan examined the frequency of use of VLSs, students' perceived usefulness of the VLSs, and the actual usefulness of the VLSs. A vocabulary test and VLS questionnaire were used to collect data. Fan found strong evidence that Hong Kong learners do not favor association strategies for imagery or grouping in learning L2 vocabulary and that the most proficient students used more strategies more often than did the less proficient students. An additional interesting finding was the complexity of VLS use in lack of consistent correlation between a given strategy's perceived usefulness and its actual usefulness.

What You Can Do . . .

1. No vocabulary strategy or training is a substitute for knowing vocabulary.

I cannot stress this enough: There is no magic cure for not knowing enough vocabulary. Teachers need to explicitly teach as much vocabulary as reasonably feasible. Strategy training is secondary. (For further discussion of the primacy of knowing vocabulary, see Myths 1 and 8.)

2. There is no one strategy or training that is better than another.

When I do workshops, teachers are genuinely disappointed upon hearing this news. Most of us expect there to be a quick fix. The good news, however, is that we know that good learners do use a variety of strategies to successfully learn new vocabulary or to deal with unknown words in a text. The teaching implication here is that we should make our students aware of a variety of strategies. The general consensus from many studies (Brown & Perry, 1991; Cohen & Aphek, 1981; Lawson & Hogben, 1996; Sanaoui, 1995) seems to be that good language learners not only have more strategies at their command but also use them more widely and more consistently.

3. Some students are totally ignorant of strategy use; others use only a handful.

The teaching implication here is to remember who we are teaching: We are teaching individuals, not classes. This is especially true with strategies. Research has shown that learners adopt very individualistic, personalized strategies for dealing with new vocabulary. The "best learners" are those who have a set plan and follow it consistently. Therefore, a teaching implication is that we should strive to make our learners aware of as many strategies as possible and we should constantly remind students of the various options when encountering a word.

For example, when learning a list of words such as *review, valley,* and *call off,* the teacher could use the following three strategies in teaching the three words (cognitive training) and make a point of making the students aware of the process (metacognitive training):

A. Teaching the word *review:*

Use morphology (word parts). Ask learners what the parts of the word mean. Language teaching should be an interactive process, not a lecture. Let learners tell you what they know, and you add to this base when needed.

Teacher: "If you look at this word, can you see two parts? How many of you can see two parts? Can anyone see *three* parts? No, OK. Then let's find the two parts. How would you divide this word into parts? Right . . . *re-* and then *view.* Who knows the word *view*? (Usually someone knows the word.) Right . . . it means *see.* What did we learn that *re-* means? Yes, it means *again.* So if you put these together, what do you have? *See again?* Now listen to this example about some students. John says, 'Can you play tennis tonight?' and Mary answers, 'No, of course not. We have a big exam tomorrow, so I have to review the material tonight.' *Review* the material? What do you think it means?"

B. Teaching the word *valley:*

Create links that are not normally there. Use the letters in the word, the length of the word, the difficult pronunciation of the word, any-

thing about the form of the word and try to tie this into the meaning. Use visuals.

Teacher: "Can someone pronounce this word? Yes, *valley*. What is the first letter of this word? OK, it's V. [Teacher writes a huge capital letter V on the board.] Look at the shape of this letter. Can someone describe this shape? Yes, it's like a big hole. Yes, it's a big angle going down. Can someone tell us the meaning of this word in English? Yes, it is the space between two mountains. [Teacher draws two big mountains, one on either side of the existing capital letter V.] When you try to remember this word, remember the first letter of this word looks just like what the word means."

C. Teaching the word *call off*:

In a phrasal verb, sometimes you can use the base verb as a "meaning holder," but more often you can use the particle or preposition. Note that I have said "more often," not "always" or even "usually."

Teacher: "Here we have a phrasal verb. That means we have two words in this example, and the first word is a verb. Let's look at the second word here. What is it? Yes, it's the word *off*. Does *off* sound more like a positive meaning or a negative meaning? Right. It's a negative meaning, and that's what it means here. Let me give you an example of *call off*. There was a group of football players who were looking forward to their big game. They practiced and practiced and were so ready to play. However, when they got to the field on the day of the game, they saw their coach who was not smiling. The sad coach told them, 'Guys, I'm sorry to tell you this, but the other team cannot play today, and there is no time to play this game any other day this season, so I'm afraid that our game has been *called off*.' What do you think *called off* means? Lost? Well, no, it's not lost because they did not play the game. No one won or lost. Anyone else? Postponed? No, postpone means you play the game later, but the coach said there was no game. Canceled? Yes, that's right. To *call off* something means to cancel it. Remember that *off* is a negative meaning in the expression *call off*, which means to cancel."

4. Your students may have strategies that are related to their cultural background or educational background. If these strategies are successful, then encourage their use—even if it goes against what you would normally do or how you were taught.

The example that comes to mind here is in teaching groups that are accustomed to rote learning of vocabulary lists, including—in my own teaching experience—Japanese, Chinese, Taiwanese, Kuwaiti, and Saudi (and many other) students. In the last three decades, memorization has been discouraged in our educational system. However, just because our system advocates one particular technique does not mean that it is as effective in other educational settings as it may be here.

Even at the lowest proficiency level, vocabulary experts such as Nation (1993) advocate a "vocabulary flood," which would entail memorizing many vocabulary items quickly. If your students do not mind this method and in fact seem to prefer it, then why not take advantage of this preference? Keep in mind the old saying: "If it's not broken, don't fix it!" I think that is sage advice here.

5. Teach learners how to keep a *neat and spacious* vocabulary notebook.

Each learner is an individual. I mention a vocabulary notebook specifically for two reasons. As a successful L2 learner, keeping a vocabulary notebook has always been a very useful strategy for me. Second, it is a concrete method that has many variations; thus, students can adapt the idea of a record of new vocabulary as they see fit, but the basic strategy is still a good one. (See Schmitt and Schmitt [1995] for an excellent article combining theory and practicality regarding learning vocabulary in general and keeping a good vocabulary notebook in particular.)

There are different ways to organize a vocabulary notebook. Since what is important to ultimate vocabulary learning here is not so much what is written down initially but rather the number of times that the learner goes back and reviews, or retrieves, information, I stress that the notebook should be as neat and spacious as possible. Neat is important because no one wants to look a second time at a messy notebook.

In addition, spacing is important. Having lots of open white space is an inviting look, one that improves the chances of the learner revisiting the page to practice retrieving meaning or form of the new words. In addition, having lots of open white space allows the learner a place to jot down subsequent information about each word. For example, a Spanish-speaking ESL student might jot down the word *make* in his or her notebook and in the far right margin put the translation *hacer*. The problem that a Spanish-speaking student has with this (and many languages—including Japanese, French, and German) is that both *make* and *do* are translated as the very same word in these L1s. At some point after writing the entry for *make* = *hacer*, the ESL student learns that *make* is for sandwiches and reservations, so the learner can go back and add this information next to the original entry for *make*—but only if enough space was left for this purpose.

6. Teach learners how to keep a vocabulary notebook in such a way it actually promotes student retrieval practice.

What does this mean? We know that one of the very most important factors in learning a word is the number of times that the learner retrieves it. These retrievals could be with form of the word, a synonym of the word, the translation of the word English → L1, the translation of the word L1 → English, a note about the word (*paws*: "used only for animals"), or a contextual example of the word.

I always cringe when I hear of teachers who make their students copy dictionary definitions of words in their vocabulary notebooks. Not only is this time consuming, it is actually unproductive and extremely unmotivating. Sanaoui's research (1995, 1996) showed that the best learners were those who followed a "structured approach" toward vocabulary learning, meaning that they had a "plan" and stuck to it. Leeke and Shaw (2000) surveyed 121 nonnative postgraduate students in the U.K. regarding their actual vocabulary learning actions and found that the optimal listing procedure is one that takes an amount of time that the learner is willing to put in. In other words, if the vocabulary notebook requires too much work, often in the form of too much information or time, students will abandon this, resulting in greatly diminished learning. L1 dictionary entries are often long, non–user friendly, and incomprehensible.

What students should do is lay out their vocabulary in a way that allows them to have multiple ways of retrieving the word. This is crucial to ultimate success in learning of many vocabulary items. One way to do this is to include these four pieces of information:

- the target word
- a translation
- a synonym or antonym or key connecting word
- and a brief example. Remember that the brief example should not be a whole sentence; all you need is a good collocation.

Here is an example of notebook entries for three vocabulary words written by a Spanish-speaking ESL student. Notice how the student has skipped a line between vocabulary entries and clearly lined up the information in two distinct columns.

Example of Student Vocabulary Notebook Entries

1. come up with
  produce or make (an answer)
	resultar en, dar un resultado
	  _____ a great solution

2. a valley
  space between 2 mountains
	valle
	  a beautiful green _____

3. commit
  make or do (smthg. negative)
	hacer, suceder
	  _____ a robbery

How does this layout encourage and facilitate student opportunities for retrieval of the vocabulary? With this design, the four pieces of information about each entry are in the same place on the page—e.g., the translation is always in the top right corner of each entry and the collocation example is always in the bottom right.

The first four retrieval possibilities are vertical pairings that allow the following question/prompt-to-answer pairings: (1) word → synonym, (2) synonym → word, (3) translation → collocation, and (4) collocation → translation. To do any of these four, learners must fold the page vertically so that only one column—i.e., the entire left column (for #1 and #2) or the entire right column (for #3 or #4)—is visible. Learners should then cover the entire column with another piece of paper or large card.

To retrieve an English synonym or definition of the vocabulary, students should fold the right column under the left column so that only half of the page (vertically) is visible—i.e., the left half. Students then cover up everything in the column except the very top word and work their way down the page exposing only the vocabulary word at first, pausing to recall/retrieve the synonym, and then pulling the cover down to expose the correct answer. To retrieve the target word from the synonym, learners start with the last vocabulary item on the page and reverse the process moving upward on the page.

To practice retrievals of a translation from a collocation or vice-versa, the same procedures should be done on the right-hand column (with the left-hand column invisible). Again, spacing and neatness are important because these allow for all eight of these retrievals to be accomplished easily.

The other four retrieval possibilities are horizontal pairings that allow the following question/prompt-to-answer pairings: (1) word → translation, (2) translation → word, (3) synonym → collocation, and (4) collocation → synonym. To do any of these four, learners should create a special cover-up card or sheet of paper that is missing one corner (one-fourth). It should look like this:

The shape of this card allows learners to cover up everything except one of the four pieces of information. To retrieve the target word from a translation, students place the card as in the illustration over their notebooks, leaving only the translation exposed. Students then work their way down the page exposing only the translation at first, pausing to recall/retrieve the word, and then pulling the cover down to expose the correct answer. To retrieve the translation from the target vocabulary word, learners turn the card over so that the opening is in the top left side and repeat the process. To practice retrievals of a synonym from a collocation or vice-versa, the same procedures should be done by inverting the covering card.

The best dictionary for second language learners is a monolingual dictionary.

AFTER MORE THAN TWO DECADES OF learning foreign languages, I do not own a single monolingual dictionary. In all of my language studies, I have used a bilingual dictionary. To be sure, some of these were more useful than others. In addition, some of these were more difficult to understand.

Using an English-English dictionary seems relatively straight-forward. Skills needed to look up the correct meaning of a word include alphabetizing, using guide words, understanding the part of speech, interpreting pronunciation symbols, and determining the most appropriate meaning of a word.

Teachers of young learners are dealing with learners who most likely have no or very limited dictionary skills in their L1. Thus, transfer of skills is not an issue because the teacher will be starting from scratch with these learners. What about transfer with adult learners, who know how to use a dictionary in their native language?

Most of the ESL teachers that I know who speak at least one foreign language know a Romance language (usually Spanish or French) or a Germanic language (usually German). Dictionary use in these languages is very similar to that of English. However, I came across very difficult dictionary issues when I was learning Arabic and Japanese.

In a class I was taking in a Japanese as a Second Language (JSL) program in Tokyo, the teacher gave us a small writing assignment. We had to write approximately ten sentences about ourselves. Having had many years of second language learning and teaching experience, this task seemed quite normal. In fact, I thought it was quite lenient. Almost immediately, the students in the class practically revolted. They were complaining about how hard this task was. I soon learned why they complained.

Japanese uses three writing systems: hiragana, katakana, and kanji. Hiragana and katakana are syllabaries. In a **syllabary**, a symbol is used for what we in English would consider a whole syllable. For example, in these two systems, there is a symbol for *ka*, for *ki*, for *ke*, for *ko*, and for *ku*. There is no symbol for just *k*. The kanji are from Chinese and are symbols that can have multiple pronunciations in Japanese (though they, too, never represent a single "letter" as in Indo-European languages).

All three of these systems can be used in the same sentence. In general, kanji is used for most words, hiragana is used for word endings and syntactic functions, and katakana is used for foreign words. It is relatively easy to learn and read and write the symbols in hiragana and katana. However, there are literally thousands of kanji, and each one is written in a certain stroke order and may be pronounced in a small set of ways.

I remember that I wanted to write the word *country* as in "I live in Niigata Prefecture. I live in a small village in a country area." I looked up *country* in my bilingual dictionary and was given several Japanese words. I think I found three possibilities: *country* as in nation, *country* as in rural, and *country* as in old-fashioned.

I knew that I had to read all the possibilities to see which one was the best Japanese word for *country* in the context that I wanted to use it.

I could not pronounce any of the words because kanji are not phonetic—that is, they are not related to the shape or design of the kanji character. I had no idea how to write these kanji characters. After at least five minutes of study, I chose the word that I thought was the *country* that I wanted.

I went back to my small essay and carefully copied the selected kanji for *country*. Again, I had no idea what I was writing. I did not know how to pronounce it. I did not know how to write it (i.e., the stroke order), but I carefully copied all of the strokes that I could see.

The next step was the worst. I knew that I had to cross-reference the three words in the Japanese-English section to see if the meaning was the one that I wanted. In Japanese, looking up a kanji character is a bit of a chore. Since these characters do not have any logical sound, a learner not familiar with the character would not be able to look it up by sound. Instead, the number of strokes in a character is key. For example, a character such as 力 has two strokes, 月 has four strokes, and 花 has seven strokes. If the character has seven strokes, the learner turns to the seven-stroke section in the dictionary. At that point, characters are arranged by "radicals" (i.e., basically, the left side of the kanji) and the roots (the main part of the kanji). It takes some time to scroll up and down a page to find the exact kanji. Needless to say, this is not an easy process. After completing the short essay, I turned in my paper.

Our JSL instructor was excellent. She had a great deal of patience as well as good teaching and people skills. About three days later, she returned our essays. My paper had a circle around the kanji that I had copied from the dictionary. Evidently, I had not chosen the correct one. At the time the paper was returned, I could not recall what I had been trying to look up when I wrote the essay. After some time, I remembered that my target had been the word *country*. I do not know what word I had written down; I do not know what word the teacher had written on my paper. Unfortunately, I did not learn any vocabulary that day.

How many times have you carefully marked a student's papers with sage comments and learning tips and outright rewrites of phrases and sentences only to see the student glance at the paper and then stuff it in a book? In this case, your effort was wasted. In the case of my JSL teacher, her effort was also wasted—and I actually tried to take advantage of what she had written.

Using a dictionary in any language can be complicated. In teaching dictionary skills to any second language learner, it is important to know the extent of the learner's literacy and ability in using a dictionary. What may seem so simple to us as speakers of one language is not necessarily so easy to speakers of a very different language.

What the Research Says . . .

It does not take second language learners very long to realize that their lack of vocabulary knowledge of that language results in serious comprehension problems. Therefore, it should come as no surprise that most L2 learners identify vocabulary deficiencies as their biggest problem in mastering a second language (Meara, 1980).

A major component of this vocabulary problem in L2 acquisition is the sheer size of vocabulary to be learned. Estimates of L1 lexical knowledge vary considerably and for good reason. Hazenberg and Hulstijn (1996) show clearly how complex this calculation can be, and Sternberg (1987) suggests that the typical adult has a vocabulary of tens of thousands of words in L1, and in exceptional cases, adults may have vocabularies in excess of 100,000 words in L1.

Furthermore, this lack of vocabulary knowledge is a problem across all skill areas but is especially apparent in ESL reading. Eskey (1988) found that not being able to automatically recognize the meaning of English words causes students who are good readers in their native language to do excessive guesswork in the second language and that this guessing slows down the process of reading. Laufer (1992) posits that if the optimal reading level is to be 70 percent, then the vocabulary size to aim for will be 5,000 word families. (A family for her includes all words related to a word—e.g., *observe, observation, observatory, observer, observable*—so that the 5,000 figure would be much larger if Laufer were counting actual words.) According to Pino-Silva (1993), average readers can recognize 50,000 words in their L1, but this is **at least five times greater** than the amount of vocabulary that L2 students know.

Given these circumstances, what are L2 learners to do when they encounter, as they will, an unfamiliar word? Basically, learners must choose one of three options: (1) they can skip the word and continue reading; (2) they can try to guess the meaning of the word from context; (3) they can look up the word in a dictionary. Each of these three options impacts vocabulary learning in a different way for a different reason.

The first option is simply to skip the word. If the learners skip a word, they may or may not be able to successfully complete the reading (or listening) activity. However, their ultimate success with the reading or listening activity does not affect the learning of the unknown vocabulary item. Learners who do not actively engage the word will not learn the word. It is as simple as this: learners cannot learn what they do not see or mentally "touch." If the item really has been skipped, then it has been skipped.

The second option is to make use of any context clues that may be available. If the learner decides to use context clues to figure out the meaning of a word, several things can happen. The learner may be successful. In this case, if the meaning of the word was very easy to guess, then relatively little mental effort or engagement has taken place with regard to this word, and incidental learning is unlikely. If the learner was unsuccessful at guessing a meaning, whether it was correct or not, the result is the same as if the word had been skipped—i.e., no incidental learning will take place. Whatever meaning the learner arrives at, as long as it has taken some degree of mental effort or engagement, then that meaning is the one that is likely to be retained. The problem that we saw with this in Myth 5 is that the learner will indeed remember an inferred meaning—even if it is incorrect. When using real context clues in real material—i.e., not material that was written especially for ESL learners—the learner is just as likely to guess incorrectly and remember a wrong answer for a right answer, thus requiring relearning at some point.

The third option is to look up the word in a dictionary. Here there are two possibilities because ESL learners may look up the word in a bilingual dictionary (English-Spanish or English-Japanese) or the learners may use a monolingual dictionary (English-English). Here we will discuss whether looking up words in a dictionary is a good thing for vocabulary learning and whether there is any reason to tell our students to use one type of dictionary instead of another.

Though many L2 teachers have definite preferences for one of the previous options, very little research comparing the efficacy of one of these methods over another exists despite the fact that learners constantly encounter unknown words and therefore have to deal with this situation repeatedly. In addition, what little research does exist is often contrary to what many L2 teachers may be doing in their classes.

Comparing dictionary use to no dictionary use, Knight (1994) reports that many teachers discourage the use of dictionaries, advising learners to guess at word meaning from context and to use dictionaries—bilingual or monolingual—as a last resort. Haynes and Baker (1993) note that ESL reading textbooks tend to promote guessing the meaning of an unknown word from the context over looking up the word in a dictionary. In addition, some textbooks in their survey went so far as to state that dictionary work should be *banned* from the classroom. However, whether this is a reflection of teachers' views or vice-versa is not known. Though no textbook analysis research has been done recently, there is little doubt things have not changed.

In a study of 105 learners of Spanish, Knight (1994) found that subjects who used a bilingual dictionary while reading a passage not only learned more words but also achieved higher reading comprehension scores than subjects who did not have a dictionary and therefore had to rely on guessing from context clues. The conclusion here is that teachers should encourage dictionary use (over use of context clues only).

Another interesting finding of this study involves students with low verbal ability with those with high verbal ability. Knight found that those with low verbal ability were able to improve their scores much more than the high–verbal ability students were. While low–verbal ability students used the dictionary to obtain word meaning, the high–verbal ability students appeared to use context to formulate an idea of the meaning and then check their dictionaries to verify their guesses. Thus, different students may need to be taught different strategies with respect to dictionary use.

In a study of 293 Japanese EFL students, Luppescu and Day (1993) examined the effect that the use of bilingual dictionaries had on overall reading comprehension. Students were given a passage to read without any time limit. Half of the students had access to bilingual dictionaries; the other half did not. All students were given a test at the end of the reading, but they were not told in advance that there would be a test. In an initial pilot testing of 27 key vocabulary items, those items known by more than half of the students were eliminated. Thus, any growth in scores between the dictionary group and the no dictionary group can be attributed to learning that took place through the use of a bilingual dictionary.

In this study, the mean measures of the dictionary group were about 50 percent greater than those of the no dictionary group. These data support the claim that the use of a bilingual dictionary can increase vocabulary learning. However, it should be noted that some test items were actually more difficult for the dictionary group. It was concluded that dictionaries may have a confusing effect on students when there are a large number of entries for a given word—that is, it is polysemous. In addition, students who used a dictionary took much more time to read the passage than those who did not use one.

Luppescu and Day (1993) note that though teachers have definite views on what kind of dictionaries should be used during reading, these views are not based on any empirical evidence. There is a serious gap in second language acquisition research here, especially given the widespread use of dictionaries in the second language learning environment.

In Folse (2001), I surveyed teachers' preferences for student strategies when encountering an unknown English word. This research study was motivated by the numerous "folktales" often heard from L2 teachers concerning L2 dictionary use. L2 teachers often make statements such as, "I don't allow my students to bring bilingual dictionaries in the room," "If students look up the word themselves, they'll remember it better," or "The students' goal ought to be to use an English-English dictionary as soon as possible because this will help them acquire English faster." However, where are the data to back up these statements?

To document L2 teachers' preferences regarding (1) dictionary use versus using context clues and (2) type of dictionary (i.e., bilingual or monolingual dictionary), an informal survey was conducted among 75 teachers on the electronic list TESL-L *(www.hunter.cuny.edu/~tesl-l/).* Teachers were asked one question, "When your students do not know a word, what kind of dictionary—English-English or bilingual—do you prefer that they use?" Teachers were free to give any answer they wanted. Most followed up their stated preference by explaining their answers at great length. Results showed that 57 percent of the teachers surveyed allow dictionary use (of any kind), 32 percent favor use of context clues to the dictionary, and 11 percent ban dictionaries, as shown in Table 9.

TABLE 9 Teachers' Preferences for Student Strategies upon Meeting an Unknown Word in Text

Preference	n	Percent
Use context clues	24	32
Allow monolingual dictionaries	28	37
Allow bilingual dictionaries	4	5
Allow different dictionary type depending on learners' level	6	8
Allow students to choose the type of dictionary	5	7
Do not allow any dictionaries	8	11
Total	75	100%

The first research question in this study was whether teachers think that it is better to have students use context clues than it is to have them look up the word in a dictionary. The use of context clues is a very popular strategy among L2 teachers. As was pointed out, many ESL textbooks strongly advocate the use of context clues, often to the exclusion of dictionary use. In this study (Folse, 2001), 43 percent of teachers indicated that they thought using context clues was better (32 percent) or they actually prohibit students to use any dictionary in class (11 percent), leaving the students with no other option but context clues.

While one study (Hulstijn 1992) showed that L2 students did remember vocabulary whose meaning had been guessed from context better than for vocabulary whose meanings had been given explicitly to the students, other studies (Schatz & Baldwin, 1986; Haynes & Baker, 1993) have shown that context clues in the real world are very limited. It is true that many L2 textbooks have specific passages and sentences that practice using context clues to guess the meaning of an unknown word, but in the real world, such a nicely packaged contextual environment is rare. Thus, teachers may be training students for a skill that will ultimately not be as useful as was previously assumed. At the very least, it would not be unfair to say that the amount of class time currently dedicated to the study and practice of context clues is perhaps not at all equivalent to the actual value of this skill in real-world language encounters.

For example, read the following statements that appear on the introductory page of a U.S. government website:

Science.gov is a gateway to _____(1)_____ _____(2)_____ science information provided by U.S. Government agencies, including research and development results. GPO is a _____(3)_____ member of the *Science.gov* partnership.

The three words that have been deleted are words that an intermediate ESL student is unlikely to know. Can you guess which three words should be inserted? If your guess is not even close to the original, then it is clear that the words have few or no supporting context clues that actually tell the meaning of the word. It is important to keep in mind that an intermediate nonnative speaker will not have the English resources and skills that you have.

The three words that have been deleted are (1) *authoritative,* (2) *selected,* and (3) *proud.* You may say that this example is not good because there are too many unknown words for such a small passage, but this is exactly the plight of even the intermediate-level nonnative speaker with real world (authentic) language material. You would also be correct in saying that it is problematic to have two unknown words back to back. However, this is the situation facing our learners.

Even if the unknown word is only one of these three, the situation is still not improved. Consider this scenario:

Science.gov is a gateway to authoritative selected science information provided by U.S. Government agencies, including research and development results. GPO is a ____(3)____ member of the *Science.gov* partnership.

Even in this scenario of only one unknown word in 29, there are no context clues to help. The only way to know that not knowing this word does not really matter here is—ironically—to know the word and its value to the passage! (Source: *www.gpoaccess.gov.* Retrieved on January 17, 2004.)

Another problem with using context clues involves an important aspect of the very goal of using context clues: *vocabulary learning.* Teachers often tell a student to use the context to guess the meaning of a word. However, the same student who does not know word X is also unlikely to know many of the words around X, supposing that such contextual clues actually exist given the situation described in the preceding paragraph. In other words, in order to have a good chance of guessing a given word, students may already need to know many of the words around it, and if they knew these words, they might also already know the word in question, in which case this whole scenario would not even exist.

A further problem is that even native speakers are not that good at guessing from context when the unknown words are low frequency words (Schatz & Baldwin, 1986). If a native speaker cannot guess the meaning of the word from the context in which it naturally occurred, then how can a nonnative speaker be expected to do so? Perhaps the use of context clues is not the "easy" skill that many teachers once assumed.

Consider the lack of any contextual support to help a **native** speaker guess the meaning of the word *extant* in the first excerpt on literature and the word *petulant* in the second example describing a movie:

Example 1:
As one example of Ovid's influence on Western art and literature, read the famous story of Daedalus and Icarus in Book 8. Ovid's account is the earliest in extant literature, although the story is much older, found on 6th century vases. Christopher Marlowe alludes to this story in his tragedy of *Dr. Faustus*, comparing his protagonist's ambition to that of Icarus. (Source: *http://larryavisbrown. homestead.com/*. Retrieved January 17, 2004.)

Example 2:
Anakin and Obi-Wan are hired to protect Amidala, whose life is threatened. Along the way, Anakin falls in love with her, slaughters several aliens and finds himself battling to be a good Jedi—one who isn't supposed to love or hate. But he does love the fair, abeit boring, Amidala. And somehow, she overcomes his unctuous, petulant character to fall in love with him. Starheads know, of course, that the pairing is necessary to produce offspring who will become Luke Skywalker and Princess Leia. (Source: *www.lasvegasweekly.com/2002/global_images/logo.gif*. Retrieved on January 17, 2004.)

The notion that context clues are extremely useful to L2 students in inferring the meaning of an unknown word comes from a potentially flawed analogy with L1. The vast majority of L1 words were not learned explicitly; they were acquired naturally from context. However, a huge difference between L1 and L2 is that the L1 speaker not only has native mastery of the syntactic patterns and the cultural background knowledge of the material in the passage (to use reading as an example), he or she also probably knows almost every word in that passage. In other words, the L1 speaker is able to use context clues so efficiently because there is only one unknown word and all of the other words present the native speaker with a solid context. The L2 learner, on the other hand, has none of these linguistic luxuries.

The second research question in this study involved the type of dictionary that L2 students should use to find the meaning of unknown words. Teachers tend to have definite beliefs about this issue in spite of the fact that there is no evidence addressing this question. Teachers who favor monolingual dictionaries comprised the largest single group. In fact, of all teachers who favored some kind of dictionary, almost 65 percent of these favored a monolingual dictionary. Another large group said that the type of dictionary to be used depends on the proficiency level of the learner—i.e., lower-proficiency learners use bilingual dictionaries and higher-proficiency students use monolingual dictionaries. Many teachers who do not allow bilingual dictionaries do so only for low-level students, stating that using a monolingual dictionary should be the goal of their learners.

Many teachers do not like bilingual dictionaries, citing problems of various kinds. Some teachers complain that the translation is the wrong one based on the context. In other words, students have selected the wrong translation from several given for a particular L2 word. However, this problem is not a dictionary problem as much as it is a question of understanding that a given word—in L1 or L2—may have several meanings that are quite different from and independent of each other. Surely this problem is not a bilingual dictionary problem as much as it is a general dictionary problem. Students need to be taught that some words, in fact many words, are polysemous and that care should be taken in selecting the proper meaning—i.e., translation from those listed. In fact, this problem is not unique to bilingual dictionaries. The exact same problem can and does happen with monolingual dictionaries.

Many of these same teachers advocate the use of monolingual dictionaries, claiming that monolingual dictionaries should be used by students as soon as possible. A purported benefit is increased English proficiency as an outgrowth of increased exposure to English. However, the kind of English that is in most dictionaries is rather special in that it consists of definitions, single words, and short phrases. The amount of increased L2 proficiency that could result from this particular kind of linguistic input cannot be that great. It is likely that even the most avid L2 learner makes far too little use of a dictionary for this effect to take place.

Interestingly, one teacher summed up the situation well when he noted that what he tells his students, which is that they ought to use a monolingual dictionary, is not what he himself does with his own foreign language studies. Many teachers, both experienced and inexperienced, are making strong statements about dictionary use when they themselves in fact either do not follow this advice or have not studied a foreign language and therefore cannot relate to what their students are going through.

In contrast, some L2 teachers support the use of bilingual dictionaries when students encounter an unknown word. The limitations of this kind of dictionary are not so different from the limitations of any kind of dictionary. One potential confounding variable in teachers' attitudes toward use of bilingual dictionaries may be the teachers' ability to use the L1. Perhaps L2 teachers who are not familiar with the L1 are threatened by the use of L1 in the classroom. In addition, L2 teachers who ban the use of L1 in their class will likely be against the use of bilingual dictionaries as well. It is understandable that teachers are trying to promote use of the L2, but if the goal is vocabulary learning and if bilingual glosses result in better learning (Chun & Plass, 1996; Knight, 1994; Hulstijn, 1993; Grace, 1998; Hulstijn 1992; Laufer & Hulstijn, 1998; Laufer & Shmueli, 1997; Prince, 1995), then why not let students use a bilingual dictionary if they wish to do so? (This is not the same as letting students speak L1 unfettered in class.)

Regardless of which type of dictionary *teachers* favor, it behooves all L2 teachers to note that little research has been done on the efficacy of a particular type of dictionary for student vocabulary learning. The extant research on first language or second language word glosses favors first language translation glosses over second language glosses. Despite the results found in this informal survey of teachers' attitudes toward student use of dictionaries, especially the bias against bilingual dictionaries, there is no empirical evidence showing that bilingual dictionaries do anything but aid comprehension and contribute to overall lexical growth and acquisition.

One final note is the use of a relatively new type of dictionary, a *bilingualized dictionary*. This kind of dictionary is actually a semi-bilingual dictionary. The L2 entry is usually followed by an L2 definition, an L1 translation, and an L2 example sentence or phrase. Thus, a bilingualized dictionary provides what a good monolingual dictionary provides (i.e., not only a definition but also a collocation) in addition to a translation. The few studies conducted on this type of dictionary have produced positive results (Laufer & Hadar, 1997; Laufer & Kimmel, 1997).

What You Can Do . . .

1. Teachers should continue to teach context clues and understand the critical limitations of context clues—but not in lieu of vocabulary itself.

In the world outside the classroom, even without any teacher's guidance, L2 learners naturally make use of whatever clues are available to them, whether they are syntactic, lexical, or contextual. However, teachers should also take into account the critical limitations of context clues that have been discussed in this book.

Many of my school positions over the years have involved supervising teachers at various types of English language programs in Saudi Arabia, in Malaysia, in Japan, and in the United States. In these positions, I have conducted hundreds of teacher observations as part of in-service training and/or evaluation. An extremely common L2 classroom interaction involves students' asking their teachers what a given word means. It is interesting to note how teachers respond to this question, particularly when students are reading a passage by themselves. The scenario—one that I have observed far too many times—goes something like this:

The student is reading a passage. The student encounters an unknown word, attempts to use context clues to discover its meaning, is unsuccessful, and then consults a dictionary. Many teachers see the use of dictionaries, especially bilingual dictionaries (which is the kind that most foreign language learners use), as unhelpful and potentially detrimental to the student's L2 growth. The teacher may see that the student is looking up a word and approaches, or the student calls for the teacher's help. The teacher comes over to help the student individually. The student points out the problematic word and asks its meaning. The teacher looks at the word, then looks at the context, and one of two things happen next.

If the word is a word that has adequate context clues (i.e., clues that will actually allow the reader to deduce the correct meaning), the teacher says, "Oh, you can figure this word out from the context clues. Try to use the context clues." With this, the teacher walks away. The student tries once again to figure out the meaning.

As both a language teacher and a language learner, this teacher response bothers me. I am not saying that it isn't appropriate at times, but the student who admits to not knowing a word does not know the word and has made an attempt to deduce its meaning. Telling the student to "do it again" is not a teaching strategy. The teacher needs to model the correct use of context clues by going through an interactive series of questions (e.g., What do you think it means? Do you think that it is something good or something bad? Is it a noun or a verb? Look at this clue. [Teacher points to a certain word.] What does this word mean? OK, it describes the first word that you asked me. Now what do you think that first word means? etc.)

If the instructor determines that knowing that word is *not* critical to understanding the main idea or any of the major secondary ideas in the passage, the teacher tells the student that the word is not important and that the student really ought to concentrate on only those words whose meaning is crucial to understanding the paragraph: "This word is not so important. Try to spend your time on the other words. Don't get bogged down with unimportant vocabulary. You don't need to know every single word to do this task." Unfortunately, many teachers fail to see the irony in this: the L2 student does not know the meaning of the word and perhaps cannot figure out the general meaning of the passage. Because of this, this student is totally incapable of determining whether or not this lexical item is important to the passage.

In other words, the student is caught in a vicious cycle. The student cannot make full use of context clues and omit an unimportant word unless he or she first knows what the word means and therefore is able to know if it is important to the passage. Knowing the word would eliminate the need for using context clues, but the student needs context clues to realize this because he or she does not know the word.

It is a frustrating, non-teaching, non-learning moment for students when the teacher seems to brush off their vocabulary (or any) questions. A question is a teachable moment; we cannot afford to waste it.

2. Teach context clues but not at the expense of explicit teaching of vocabulary.

If context clues are to be useful, learners will need a great deal of vocabulary in order to understand enough of the surrounding context with which to work. Perhaps some of the class time currently devoted to teaching the use of context clues would be better spent on explicit teaching and learning of vocabulary.

3. Teachers should be aware that the real value of teaching context clues may not necessarily be in the learning of using context clues per se but rather in better overall English proficiency.

To be certain, practicing context clues makes learners more aware of certain types of context clues. However, what may be more important than the learning of a particular type of context clue, which may have limited value in the real world, is the additional language experience or syntactic solidification or even moving in the reading process from individual words to "chunking." It could also be well argued that exercises that use controlled language to work with context clues are actually a form of comprehensible input since the input has been carefully controlled so as to make sure that all of the words except the particular vocabulary item being practiced are known by learners at this L2 proficiency level.

4. Relatively few words are learned through incidental acquisition; drawing learners' attention to words enhances vocabulary retention.

Teachers need to remember that incidental vocabulary acquisition is not a given; it is dependent on many factors, such as the saliency of the word to the meaning of the passage or completion of the assignment or task. As a result, teachers should not expect learners to pick up vocabulary simply because it is there. Empirical evidence shows that incidental vocabulary acquisition occurs when the learner needs to notice that unknown word—i.e., a sort of consciousness-raising occurrence. If teachers want students to remember certain words, then teachers need to provide specific and explicit activities and tasks that will make learners take notice of the words.

5. Teachers must stop saying emphatically that the goal of L2 learners is to move toward the use of a monolingual dictionary as quickly as possible.

There is absolutely no empirical evidence—quantitative or qualitative—to support the familiar notion that monolingual dictionaries are better than bilingual dictionaries for understanding and learning L2 vocabulary. Research has examined the use of L1 versus L2 in glossing in small experiments, but there have been no long-term investigations (i.e., the length of the language course) comparing the language proficiency of L2 learners who used a monolingual dictionary with those who used a bilingual dictionary in actual L2 classes. In fact, the whole issue of dictionaries in second language acquisition has been surprisingly untouched in research.

6. Dictionaries are a part of the language learning process and are here to stay.

Krashen (1989) notes that learners carry around their dictionaries with them, not their grammar books. Rather than fight their use, especially in the light of the paucity of hard evidence to support this negative view, teachers ought to concentrate on taking full advantage of this valuable learning tool. Learners in particular need to understand that consulting a dictionary may at times be a more efficient method of dealing with unknown vocabulary.

7. Teachers must teach students how to deal with polysemous words.

Many words in English have multiple meanings. When learners come across an unknown word in a reading passage and look it up in a dictionary (monolingual or bilingual), they are then faced with the question of deciding which meaning they should select. This skill is not as common as might be thought. It is worth explicitly teaching and practicing this skill. In addition to improving lookup results with polysemous words, students will also learn valuable vocabulary if the teacher or textbook author has chosen high-frequency words.

A typical example is to have a dictionary entry with all the meanings followed by several sentences in which the various meanings of the word are exemplified. Students have to indicate which of the multiple meanings is being used in each sentence. An example from *Intermediate Reading Practices, 3rd Edition* (Folse, 2004c), is shown.

Dictionary Usage: Definitions and Contexts

Exercise: Read this entry, and answer the questions by placing a check (✓) by the correct answer.

> *form* (fōrm) *n.* 1. The shape or structure of something. 2. A variety or kind of: a form of ocean life. 3. A paper or application with blanks for information. 4. Condition, especially about health or fitness 5. A change in a word. *vt* 1. Make or shape. 2. Organize. *vi* Take shape; develop [Middle English *forme, fourme,* from Old French, from Latin *forma,* form, shape]

Choose the meaning or context that *form* has in each sentence:

4. Please complete this *form*.

     _____ n.1   _____ n.2   _____ n.3   _____ n.4   _____ n.5

5. He won because he was in excellent *form*.

     _____ n.1   _____ n.2   _____ n.3   _____ n.4   _____ n.5

6. Did you learn those irregular verb *forms*?

     _____ n.1   _____ n.2   _____ n.3   _____ n.4   _____ n.5

7. A circle is a *form*.

     _____ n.1   _____ n.2   _____ n.3   _____ n.4   _____ n.5

8. Perhaps there is some *form* of life on the moon.

     _____ n.1   _____ n.2   _____ n.3   _____ n.4   _____ n.5

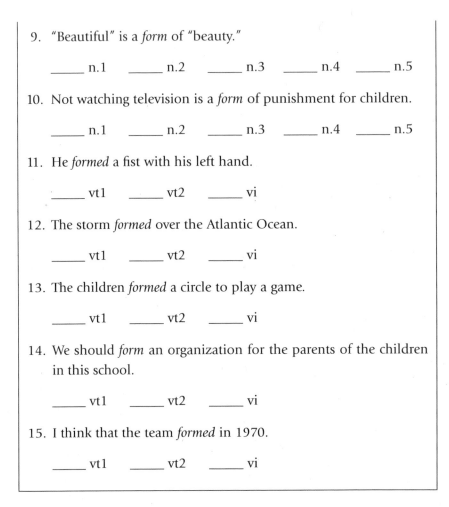

9. "Beautiful" is a *form* of "beauty."

_____ n.1 _____ n.2 _____ n.3 _____ n.4 _____ n.5

10. Not watching television is a *form* of punishment for children.

_____ n.1 _____ n.2 _____ n.3 _____ n.4 _____ n.5

11. He *formed* a fist with his left hand.

_____ vt1 _____ vt2 _____ vi

12. The storm *formed* over the Atlantic Ocean.

_____ vt1 _____ vt2 _____ vi

13. The children *formed* a circle to play a game.

_____ vt1 _____ vt2 _____ vi

14. We should *form* an organization for the parents of the children in this school.

_____ vt1 _____ vt2 _____ vi

15. I think that the team *formed* in 1970.

_____ vt1 _____ vt2 _____ vi

8. Consider allowing your students to use a bilingualized dictionary.

This type of learner dictionary is most definitely user-friendly. It provides the most information appealing to a wide variety of individual learner differences. Students who prefer to use a monolingual dictionary can find the information that they wanted but can also verify their answer through the translations. Students who prefer a bilingual dictionary still have access to L1 translations. All students have access to an example sentence or phrase that illustrates a good collocation usage.

MYTH

Teachers, textbooks, and curricula cover second language vocabulary adequately.

In the Real World . . .

PART OF BEING A GOOD LANGUAGE TEACHER is being able to empathize with your students and understand their language needs. With this in mind, I proposed a new elective course at an intensive academic English program at a university where I was teaching. The course was eight weeks long and consisted of one 50-minute class per day. Thus, there were 40 hours of class time. In this program, students had five hours of class per day: three hours of core courses and two hours of electives. This particular course was aimed at the upper-proficiency students, what many instructors would recognize as "upper intermediate" and "advanced" proficiency.

Because I strongly believed that our students needed more vocabulary, I proposed a course that would attempt to teach students approximately 25 words per day. Given that the class was only 50 minutes long, this class would have to be more teacher-centered than most current classes. In addition, the bulk of the work would definitely fall on the students, who had to absorb so many words so quickly. I recall that there was some discussion from the curriculum supervisors regarding the wisdom of a course that seemed to violate so many of the "common sense" principles that were in vogue at that time. There was a lot of material to learn in a short period, the students would not have much time for talk, and the pace would have to be rather brisk to say the least.

For this course, I chose to use a book called *Vocabulary in Use* (Cambridge University Press) because it was the only book at that time that had enough vocabulary arranged in chunks. Although many of the units are organized into semantic sets, which we have seen in Myth 3 to be a hindrance in second language vocabulary learning, there are many units that are organized in other ways. The layout of the book was simple. Each unit consisted of two facing pages: one page of words and teaching on the left and a facing page of brief exercises on the right. This design was a good match for an intensive course being taught at such a brisk pace. (*Note:* This type of format would not match everyone's curriculum, so teachers should plan accordingly.)

For the 40-day course, I chose 35 lessons from the book. (The extra five days were taken up by exams and school functions.) I chose the vocabulary groups that seemed the most important to my students. I chose units such as "Distances and Dimensions," "Cause, Reason, Purpose, and Result," and "Expressions with *Come* and *Go*." As presented in Myth 3, it is not good to teach words that are similar in meaning at the same time, but with students at this higher-proficiency level, they knew many of the target words already. Most of the time, they were learning one of the words in a pair or set, so they were able to focus on only one word and the differences between it and the already known word.

Teaching this kind of course is very demanding. The teacher has to be very energetic and very enthusiastic in order to maintain the students' interest and keep them focused for the entire class period. The teacher must be someone who is able to explain things rapidly and unexpectedly—when the student asks you out of the blue what the difference is between X word and Y word. The teacher must be someone who

Myth 8: Teachers, textbooks, curricula . . . / 129

is able to come up with numerous examples of the word that represent real usage and that are meaningful to the students. Finally, the teacher must be someone who has lots of different learning activities in his or her bag of tricks, since he or she may have to do a quick oral matching activity or an odd-man-out game on the spot. (An outstanding source of ideas for teaching vocabulary is *New Ways in Teaching Vocabulary* [Nation, P. 1994. Alexandria, Va.: TESOL].)

What was the result of this course? I do not have any hard data on the number of words that students learned from this course, but I was able to read student comments in the course evaluations. Over and over, students said that this was the best course that they had ever taken. Many students also said that this course should not be an elective but rather a core course. In all of my 25 years of teaching English in the United States and in many different foreign countries, I had never heard anyone make this comment. The students did not like this course; they *loved* it.

The moral of this personal experience is that second language learners are very aware of the importance of vocabulary and their lack of vocabulary knowledge. This was not a particularly easy course, but students rose to the challenge and attended to the duties well enough. The final course evaluations speak for themselves. Despite the obvious success of this course, it did not become part of the permanent curriculum, and that is exactly the point of Myth 8.

What the Research Says . . .

Since the first myth in this book is that vocabulary is not as important in learning a second language as other aspects such as grammar at a theoretical level, it is appropriate that the last myth deal with the extent of vocabulary in current language course curricula, a sort of "state of the union" if you will. In Myth 1, I explain why vocabulary is more important than grammar. In Myth 8, we can look at this issue from three perspectives because "curriculum" ranges from a general plan of study to the specific exercises that we do in class. In the first perspective, we consider vocabulary in the curriculum in general, a sort of big picture. In the second perspective, we reflect on vocabulary in specific areas of the curriculum such as K–3, a middle school math class, reading, and academic composition. Last, we consider specific practice activities.

Perspective 1: Vocabulary in the Curriculum in General

The myth under consideration here is that vocabulary is covered enough in our curricula, materials, and courses. Most of us do not have to look very far to find that this is most certainly not true; vocabulary *is not* covered well enough. The support for this comes from learners themselves in two ways: how well they are able to function in the L2 and what they say about their course curricula.

One of the greatest frustrations in trying to learn any language is that important moment when you are trying to speak to a native speaker and you do not know the word that you need at that particular moment. You quickly search for another word in your brain but cannot find that one either. You try to manage in broken language, sometimes successfully but oftentimes not. The same occurs in writing. In written work, for example, learners rarely use any new vocabulary (unless told to do so); they often make do with the vocabulary that they already know. When listening to a news clip or a listening passage, learners' comprehension problems are seldom due to listening issues but rather language issues, notably vocabulary. No matter how good students' "listening" abilities are, they cannot comprehend materials that contain many words that they do not know. All second language learners can relate to the limitations of insufficient vocabulary knowledge.

In addition to our students' language production problems due to vocabulary, we also have their wishes, as expressed in student surveys. Adult L2 learners are aware of their "vocabulary plight." They see acquisition of vocabulary as their greatest source of problems (Green & Meara, 1995; Meara, 1980). In surveys of ESL students in intensive academic programs (Flaitz, 1998; James, 1996; Folse 2004b), students expressed a strong desire for vocabulary instruction. In many surveys, students ranked vocabulary development second only to opportunities to speak in class. Clearly, learners believe that vocabulary is extremely important.

In spite of these issues, vocabulary is not dealt with sufficiently. Yes, some teachers cover some vocabulary, but this is hardly ever done very systematically. Vocabulary is something that everyone *assumes* that learners will somehow pick up, much the same way everyone assumes that students will just pick up good pronunciation.

In Folse (2004a), I describe results from an observation of vocabulary learning of students at an intensive English program at a university. Five consecutive days of English classes of two groups of upper-intermediate students were observed. These students had five 50-minute classes each day in grammar, reading, writing, speaking, and TOEFL. Classes were observed to note any vocabulary activity—whether teacher-initiated or student-initiated—that took place during the class.

One interesting finding was that there was no overall plan of vocabulary instruction in the curriculum. Whereas grammar had been taken into account across all levels, words were only taught as needed. Many daily class activities did not stretch students' language, and as a result, very little new vocabulary was introduced. Only a few teachers wrote new vocabulary on the board. In fact, most teachers did very little with the vocabulary. Furthermore, there was almost no follow-up practice of the new vocabulary—i.e., very little recycling.

A second finding was that the most common student language question to arise in *all* five daily classes—grammar, reading, writing, speaking, and TOEFL—was related to vocabulary. Interestingly, even in the grammar class, the most frequently asked language question was not about grammar but rather about the *vocabulary* in the lesson. This finding is especially important because ESL grammar textbooks are almost always written so that the vocabulary is almost never problematic and that the grammar will stand out more and therefore be easier to learn.

In this excerpt from page 76 of Unit 5, Adverbs of Manner and Related Terms, in my *Clear Grammar 3* (Folse 1999a), the grammar focus of the exercise is on the use of the preposition *by* versus *with* to indicate **agent**. In general, we use *by* with a means or method that involves communication or transportation, and we use *with* with other types of instruments or means. The noun following *by* is a noun without an article or plural marker; a count noun following *with* is appropriately marked for number with an article or a plural suffix.

Exercise: Write *by* or *with* on the lines.

1. *Ann:* Did you take these pictures _____ your new camera?

    Paul: Yes, I did. That's a great camera.

    Ann: But it's really expensive. How did you manage to pay for it?

    Paul: I paid for it _____ a credit card, so I still have a few weeks until I have to pay for it.

2. *Jack:* This is my first time to go to Europe.

    Hank: And you're going _____ ship. You're so lucky.

    Jack: Lucky? I wish we were going _____ plane. Traveling _____ ship does not seem so nice to me.

3. *Fran:* Staying in touch _____ telephone is certainly easier nowadays.

    Greg: I couldn't agree with you more, but my sister and I communicate _____ e-mail almost every day.

4. *Luke:* Can I pay for this _____ check?

    Clerk: You can use a check if you want. You can also pay _____ credit card.

5. *Zina:* Did Julia drive there _____ friends?

    Wes: No, they went there _____ bus.

These five mini-dialogues are fine for practicing this grammar point. In each example, there is a clearly marked place to write the grammar answer, and this answer will stand out. However, if we consider this exercise as a potential conduit for vocabulary, we can see that it in fact does not include much vocabulary. This is typical of grammar books since the purpose of the book *is* to focus on grammar.

Perhaps partially in reaction to this but more likely in reaction to recent trends toward "integrated skills" in language curricula, ESL grammar books have been "beefed up" with readings, writing activities, and even listening exercises with cassettes and CDs. The result, in my opinion, has not been good. What used to be a 150-page book now has more than 300 pages. To use the material in these newer integrated "grammar" books, the curriculum and scheduling *must* be adjusted so that this book would then be not only in this one class (i.e., the grammar class) but also in the reading class and perhaps the listening class.

Along with these additional reading and listening passages come more vocabulary, which would seem to be a good thing. However, as class time is limited, the teacher must focus on the grammar. Students complain that they have to buy textbooks that we cannot cover completely in class. It was difficult to cover the grammar book material before these newer, thicker books came out; it is virtually impossible today. In addition, with all of the material in the book, it is ironic that the grammar points—supposedly the main objective of this course and textbook—tend to get lost.

A third important finding was that the class where vocabulary was covered most depended on the *instructor*, not the class subject. Reading, for example, would seem to be a class that would logically teach a lot of vocabulary. For one group of students, this was in fact the class where they learned the bulk of their vocabulary. However, for the other group, the speaking class provided their biggest source of vocabulary input because the instructor made a point of not simplifying his English too much, was aware of new vocabulary that he was using, and repeated each word before writing it on the board. If language teachers were more aware of the importance of vocabulary in second language learning and specific class activities, perhaps we would see vocabulary taught or at least addressed more consistently by more teachers.

Perspective 2: **Vocabulary in the Specific Areas of the Curriculum**

Vocabulary needs are different for different areas of the curriculum. These needs ultimately depend on the learner's background and language goals as evidenced in the following four examples: K–3 ESL, middle school math, reading, and academic composition.

In a K–3 ESL setting, some learners are bilingual, but many are still weak in their native language. In either case, lack of vocabulary certainly hinders the students' ability to understand instruction in English. What happens when the first grade teacher explains what is needed for a picnic and writes the words *picnic, basket, food, paper plate, napkins,* and *drinks* on the board next to pictures of these items? It is important for teachers with a few ESL pupils in their classes to be aware of two kinds of learning taking place. Native English-speaking children are learning the sound-letter correspondence between /pIknIk/ and the word *picnic,* whereas the ESL child has to first figure out what a picnic is, then how to pronounce it, and finally how to spell it.

In a middle school math class with some ESL learners, learning may be affected by ESL students' low test scores, which may in fact be due to vocabulary in the assessment process. In other words, the vocabulary in the assessment instrument itself may result in low scores and thus hide the fact that the learners actually know the math concept. Consider the math problem here:

How Far?

SITUATION: Maria, Sarah, Bob, Nick, and John have each made a map showing how far they live from their school.

- On Maria's map, her house is 4 inches from school. She used a scale of 1 inch = $\frac{1}{2}$ mile.
- Sarah and John both used a scale of 1 inch = $\frac{1}{4}$ mile. On their map, the distance from Sarah's house to the school is 7 inches more than the distance from John's house to the school.
- Nick used a scale where 1 inch corresponds to one mile.
- On Bob's map, his house is 3 inches from the school. Bob actually lives closer to the school than any other student.
- Maria used the same scale as Bob did.
- The distance from Nick's house to the school on his map is twice as long as the distance from Maria's house to the school on her map.
- On John's map, his house is exactly 1 inch from the school.

QUESTION: How far from school does each student live?

This math problem works with ratio, a mathematics area covered in 7th grade. Although the problem is relatively straightforward for native speakers, it is important to note that this one question actually consists of 166 words. Many of these words are in fact difficult vocabulary problems for ESL learners: *both, each, the same . . . as, close(r) (to), twice, as . . . as,* and *how far.* Not knowing one, two, or a handful of these comparison expressions greatly reduces an ESL learner's chances of solving the math problem *even if he or she knows the math concept of ratio well*—and that was the purpose of the problem!

Reading is perhaps the most fundamental language skill at all levels. Nonnative speakers must have good reading skills if they expect to have any chance of academic success. Numerous researchers (Alderson,

1984; Beck, Perfetti, & McKeown, 1982; Coady, Magoto, Hubbard, Graney, & Mokhtari, 1993; Davis, 1944; Haynes, 1993; James, 1996; Kameenui, Carnine, & Freschi, 1982; Laufer, 1992, 1997; Nation & Coady, 1988) have shown the relationship between vocabulary knowledge and reading ability.

An obvious vocabulary problem with regard to reading is the sheer size of vocabulary to be learned. Estimates of L1 lexical knowledge vary considerably and for good reason. Hazenberg and Hulstijn (1996) clearly show how complex this calculation can be, and Sternberg (1987) suggests that the typical adult has a vocabulary of tens of thousands of words in L1, and in exceptional cases, adults may have vocabularies in excess of 100,000 words in L1.

While lack of vocabulary knowledge is a problem across all skill areas, it is especially apparent in ESL reading. Exploring L1 reading, Davis (1944) studied nine components cited in the literature as involved in reading comprehension—namely knowledge of word meanings:

- ability to select the appropriate meaning according to context
- ability to follow text organization
- ability to select the main idea of a passage
- ability to answer details
- ability to answer questions that are not phrased as in the passage
- ability to draw inferences
- ability to recognize literary devices that indicate tone and mood
- ability to determine the writer's purpose and view.

Using a factorial analysis, Davis found that the first component, knowledge of word meaning, constitutes the largest element of reading comprehension.

Further evidence of the important role that the reader's lexical knowledge plays in reading ability abounds. In measures of text readability for L1 readers, lexical difficulty has repeatedly been shown to be the most significant predictor of overall readability of a passage (Nation & Coady, 1988). It is well accepted that vocabulary knowledge is crucial to reading comprehension ability (Koda, 1989; McKeown & Curtis, 1987). For obvious reasons, the importance of vocabulary knowledge is even more important in L2 than in L1.

Discussing a cognitive model of strategies that L2 learners make use of when they attempt to infer an unknown word's meaning, Huckin and Bloch (1993) point out, "Research has shown that second-language readers rely heavily on vocabulary knowledge, and that a lack of vocabulary knowledge is the largest obstacle for second-language readers to overcome" (p. 154). Likewise, Haynes and Baker (1993) found that the main obstacle for L2 readers is not lack of reading strategies but rather insufficient vocabulary knowledge in English. Laufer and Sim (1985) list these areas in order of decreasing importance in reading ability in L2: knowledge of vocabulary, subject matter, discourse markers, and syntactic structure. In sum, Laufer and Sim find that vocabulary is *most* important, syntax *least* important. In spite of this, ESL curricula do not systematically deal with vocabulary.

In addition to negatively impacting reading ability, the lack of well-planned vocabulary instruction in writing curricula affects student writing. Less research has been done on the role of vocabulary in composition, but studies have shown the effect that a large L2 vocabulary base can have on writing skills (Laufer & Nation, 1995; Laufer, 1998b). In a seminal work using 1,457 essays written by speakers of American English, Chinese, Japanese, Korean, Vietnamese, Arabic, and Indonesian, Hinkel (2001) compares differences in the way native speakers and nonnative speakers address essays based on the same writing prompts. She very clearly delineates specific differences in the way each of these two groups uses formulaic vocabulary and offers suggestions for dealing with this issue in curricula.

Perspective 3: Vocabulary in Practice Activities in the Curriculum

A third way to look at curriculum is to look at one of its smallest yet most concrete manifestations: *practice activities.* These can consist of both oral and written exercises that are designed to help learners retain new vocabulary.

There is empirical evidence that instruction needs to include associating words with definitions and that it should go well beyond this (Beck, McKeown, & Omanson, 1987; McKeown, Beck, Omanson, & Pope, 1985). Instructional conditions should be set up so as to maximize the amount of processing of words. These researchers call for "rich instruction," which should include activities that require discussion of the words and require students to create justifications for the relationships and associations that they discover. In addition, teachers should make use of activities that will specifically increase the number of times learners will encounter the words.

According to Nation (2001), the three most important components of activities that foster L2 vocabulary growth are *noticing, retrieval,* and *creative or generative use of the words.* Because these three components offer teachers and materials writers a useful checklist for evaluating the potential of classroom activities when the goal is L2 vocabulary retention, each of the three components will be discussed at some length here.

NOTICING

Noticing means that learners need to notice the word and be aware of it as a useful language item. Noticing may be affected by several factors, including the salience of the word, the learners' previous contact with the word, and the learners' realization that the word fills a gap in their knowledge of the L2. (See Schmidt [1990] for a discussion of what noticing entails and Laufer [1997] for a discussion of what noticing new L2 lexical items requires of the L2 learner.)

Noticing a word requires *decontextualization.* It is important to understand that decontextualization does not mean that there is no context. Rather, it means that the word is removed temporarily from the message context in which it occurred so that the learner can focus on the form and the meaning of the word—i.e., so that the word can be focused on as a language item.

Nation (2001) cites four examples of decontextualizing a word: learner attention or recognition of the word, teacher focus or attention on the word, negotiation of meaning of the word, and teacher explanation of the word. What does each of these mean for classroom teachers?

The first example of decontextualizing a word occurs when a learner sees or hears a new word and actually thinks about the word for a second. Perhaps the learner realizes that he or she has never run across this word at any other time. Perhaps the learner is puzzled by the usage of this word in this particular context because the meaning of the word is different from what the learner already knew for the word's meaning. (For example, the learner knows that *tire* is the round thing on a car and then runs into the phrase "Working all night will certainly *tire* you out," where *tire* is a verb, not a noun.)

The second example, which is accomplished by the teacher or textbook author, can be done in numerous ways. The teacher could write the word on the board and circle it. The teacher could say, "In the first paragraph on page 27, I want you to underline these five words." Likewise, the textbook author could have key vocabulary words in boldfaced type or underlined.

Another way to decontextualize a word is to have learners pull words out of their natural context and discuss their meanings. Here is an example of a conversation between two nonnative speakers that includes negotiation of meaning:

Marcos: What's problem for this light?

Chen: I don't know. This light good?

Marcos: I'm not sure. Maybe the bulb is finished. Do you have another?

Chen: I don't know. What means "bub"? You mean Bob?

Marcos: No, not Bob, Bulb. B-u-l-b. It's a light. Like this.

As you can see, Chen did not know the word *bulb*. He didn't know the word, and so he wasn't able to understand it when he heard it. In fact, it sounded to him like the boy's name Bob.

Negotiation of meaning has been investigated as a component in speaking activities (Doughty & Pica, 1986; Folse, 2003a; Folse & Bologna, 2003; Long, 1989; Long & Porter, 1985; Newton, 1991; Pica & Doughty, 1985a, 1985b). Studies (Ellis, Tanaka, & Yamazaki, 1994; Newton, 1995) have shown that words that are negotiated when encountered are retained much better than words that are not negotiated. Though negotiation is therefore a good thing for L2 vocabulary learning and retention, Nation (2001) points out that these studies also found that negotiation tasks take much more time than non-negotiation tasks and that negotiation may be of limited value. Newton (1995) found that negotiation items were more likely to be learned than non-negotiation items (75 percent to 57 percent) but that negotiation was responsible for about only 20 percent of the vocabulary learning. Nation (2001) highlights another interesting fact about negotiation studies: Learners observing negotiation of meaning retain vocabulary just as well as those learners who were actually involved in the negotiation (Ellis, Tanaka, & Yamazaki, 1994; Newton, 1995; Stahl & Clark, 1987). This finding has implications for teachers of large classes or teachers in cultures where classes are usually teacher-centered. It is not imperative that all learners be involved in the negotiation for learning of L2 vocabulary to take place; observing other learners also seems to suffice.

Another way to decontextualize a word is to provide a definition of a new word. Providing a definition focuses attention on the word as an individual word rather than as part of the message. Elley (1989) found that vocabulary learning is increased if the new words are briefly explained while learners are listening to a story; in fact, vocabulary retention rates were double when the new words were explained briefly.

RETRIEVAL

Retrieval is the second of the components that Nation (2001) believes can enhance L2 vocabulary retention. According to the Information

Process Model as explained by Padilla and Sung (1990), retrieval and rehearsal are central in helping move information from short-term memory to long-term memory. In the learning phase, Nation (2001) notes the sequence in which a word may be first noticed by the learner and then comprehended by the learner (whether through clues from the surrounding text or by a teacher explanation). After this, the next important step is to solidify the new word's meaning and usage in the learner's head. One way to do this is for the learner to complete tasks that require the learner to retrieve the word.

Nation (2000) points out the differences between tasks that make use of *receptive retrieval* and those that require *productive retrieval*. Receptive retrieval requires the learners to retrieve the meaning of a word that is seen (in reading) or heard (in listening). Here the learners are able to retrieve the meaning of a word that was produced by someone else. In productive retrieval, the learners must actually want to use the word and then produce the word in their own speaking or writing. One very important caveat that Nation (2001) notes is that retrieval does *not* occur when the form and the meaning of a word are presented at the same time.

In this exercise from *Intermediate Reading Practices, 3rd edition* (Folse, 2004c), students are practicing *receptive retrieval* because they do not have to retrieve the actual word *turbulent* since it is given in the question:

---

10. What does the word *turbulent* mean here?

It was a very <u>turbulent</u> flight. In fact, the pilot told all the passengers to sit down, buckle their seatbelts, and remain seated for the rest of the flight. The flight attendants were not allowed to serve any food or drinks, and no one was able to go to the restroom even.

    A. an underground passage
    B. soft powder used in baking
    C. violent movement in air flow (Lesson 5, Ex. 7)

The next example is an example of *productive retrieval*. Here learners actually have to come up with the target word. This example is from Exercise 3 of Lesson 5 of *Intermediate Reading Practices, 3rd edition* (Folse, 2004c):

---

5. There is no _____ between the word *sea* and *see*. The verb *see* is not related to the noun *sea*. [answer: relationship, connection]

Teachers can also do rapid-fire reviews of the previous day's vocabulary words by asking questions such as, "What is the word we learned yesterday that means 'twelve' of something?" [answer: dozen] or "What do you call the card or paper that you get when you want to be able to drive a car?" [answer: license, driver's license]

It is important not to confuse repetition with retrieval. *Repetition* is simply encountering the word more than one time. In *retrieval*, however, the learners are actually required to "pull up" the meaning of the word. When learners hear or see a new word, they need an activity (or a strategy) that will later force them to retrieve the meaning of the word (multiple times ideally).

Several researchers (Atkins & Baddeley, 1998; Baddeley, 1990) stress the importance of not only retrieval but the number of retrievals and the timing of the retrievals because each retrieval strengthens the neurological link between the form of the word and its corresponding meaning. It is believed that the stronger this link is, the easier subsequent retrievals are.

One final point is that research (Atkins & Baddeley, 1998; Baddeley, 1990; Pimsleur, 1967) also indicates that retrieval is most effective when the intervals between retrievals gradually increase. In other words, there would be a rather short interval between the initial learning of a word and its meaning and the next retrieval of the word's meaning, but this interval would gradually increase between subsequent meetings. (For an overview of research on rehearsal regimes, see

Hulstijn, 2001. For more detailed information on rehearsal regimes, see Bahrick, Bahrick, Bahrick, & Bahrick, 1993; Bjork, 1988; Landauer & Bjork, 1978.)

CREATIVE OR GENERATIVE USE

Creative or generative use of new words is the third component of Nation's (2001) list of components for enhancing word retention. Creative or generative use of a word refers to using the word in a way that is different from the original encounter. For example, if the learners encountered the word *freeze* in the sentence "Water will freeze at 32 degrees Fahrenheit" and then "The computer will freeze if you run too many programs at the same time," they will have to retrieve the meaning that they had assigned to *freeze* (i.e., change from liquid to ice) and then test it out in the new situation.

Nation (2001) explains how there are degrees of generation. If the linguistic context for the target word is not so different from the original input, then creative or generative use is low. If the target word is *squander*, then moving from "He squandered the money" to "He squandered a lot of money" represents little creative or generative use. On the other hand, moving from "He squandered the money" to "He squandered an opportunity" represents much more creative or generative use of the target word. In addition, high (or innovative) creative or generative use simultaneously requires retrieval.

What Kind of Exercises Are Best for Practicing Vocabulary and Why?

Unfortunately, the short answer to this question is that there has been up to now very little research conducted on the specific question of what type or types of exercises actually enhance vocabulary retention. Some have believed that what is important is not the kind of written practice but rather that learners undertake any form of written practice.

Perhaps due to the dearth of empirical research on exercise types, coursebooks make use of an extremely wide variety of types of exercises, including fill-in-the-blank, multiple choice, matching, short answer, and problem solving. Kameenui, Dixon, and Carnine (1987) make a distinction between exercises that require *label-to-concept* processing and those that deal with *concept-to-label* processing. Multiple choice exercises frequently make use of concept-to-label processing:

> *Maria got ahead in life quickly because she was so* _____.
> *(a) ambitious   (b) trivial   (c) dreadful*

The authors make a strong case promoting the use of label-to-concept processing:

> *Jamie believed her father wanted her to be more ambitious.*
> *What are some things that <u>ambitious</u> people do?*

The authors also promote visual-spatial displays and graphic organizers that help learners understand content textbook passages, something that is especially important for K–12 ESL learners. The authors do not show any preference as to whether these should be included in actual L2 exercises or if they should be taught as learning strategies. Either would seem to suffice.

Though fill-in-the-blank exercises are commonly used, Sciarone and Meijer (1995) found in their study that blank-filling exercises do not contribute more to acquisition than conversation practice. This does not mean, however, that teachers should abandon completion exercises for conversation practice. Their conclusion is that it is more likely that there is no strong reason to do only *one* of these exercises to the exclusion of the other.

The number of types of vocabulary exercises is seemingly endless, and teachers should note why each may be beneficial for the learner. It is important to see how a simple modification in the directions and/or design of an exercise controls the number of retrievals a student has to perform and whether the task is *receptive retrieval* or *productive retrieval*. In other words, the teacher can make a small change that in essence requires the learner to "touch" the words in a different way, which can result in better retention of the vocabulary, as illustrated in Table 10.

TABLE 10 Teacher Manipulation of Design and Student Directions

Vocabulary Exercise	Design and Directions	Type of Learning Transaction
Matching	2 columns of 10 items; left column is the vocabulary; right column is definition. "Write the letter of the definition in the right column next to the corresponding vocabulary in the left column."	Receptive retrieval
Matching	2 columns of items; left column has 10 vocabulary; right column has 14 definitions. The 4 distractors are actual definitions from the lesson, too. "Write the letter of the definition in the right column next to the corresponding vocabulary in the left column. There are 4 definitions that you will not use."	Receptive retrieval of 10 items; optional but likely productive retrieval of 4 items (I found that some of the best retained words were those that were never a correct answer in any exercise, as the 4 distractor definitions are here [Folse 1999].)
Matching	2 columns of items; left column has 14 vocabulary; right column has 10 definitions. The 4 distractors are actual words from the lesson, too. "Write the letter of the definition in the right column	Receptive retrieval of 10 items; optional but likely productive retrieval of 4 items (Again, the 4 distractor words serve a useful purpose. Though

	next to the corresponding vocabulary in the left column. There are 4 words that do not have a definition. Leave these blank."	learners do not have to mentally retrieve these words' definitions, most learners cannot help doing this.)
Defining	1 column of 10 vocabulary followed by a blank space. "Write a good definition for each of the vocabulary words."	Productive retrieval of the definition
Labeling	1 column of 10 definitions preceded by a blank line. "Write the vocabulary word that is defined."	Productive retrieval of the vocabulary word

Too often we tend to limit ourselves to two or three traditional kinds of exercises, but there are numerous permutations of vocabulary exercises. The following list is a brief sample of some vocabulary exercise possibilities (Table 11):

TABLE 11 Examples and Permutations of Exercise Type

Exercise	Directions and Example Items (Note: italicized words are the target/studied vocabulary.)
True-false (or yes-no)	"Read the statement and write true or false on the line." 1. ____ If you have a *dozen* cookies, you have ten of them. 2. ____ If you touch the *blade* of a knife, you might cut yourself.

Odd-man out (only one word was recently studied; others are assumed known)	"Circle the word that is different from the other three." 1. beetle approach bee *caterpillar* 2. pilot *slender* waiter receptionist
Odd-man out (all 4 words were recently studied)	"Circle the word that is different from the other three." 1. *beetle approach mosquito caterpillar* 2. *thin slender skinny portrait*
Cloze sentences (unrelated sentences)	"Fill in the blanks with one of these 10 words: *army, cattle, donkey, foe, ivory, lament, oath, portray, tortoise, venom.*" 1. Sometimes a snake's _____ can kill a human being. 2. When a soldier comes across an unknown person, he or she has to determine if the unknown person is friend or _____.
Cloze passage (related sentences)	"Fill in the blanks with one of these 10 words: *army, cattle, donkey, foe, ivory, lament, oath, portray, tortoise, venom.*" Snakes have a bad reputation, but they do not seek to attack. When a snake comes across an unknown object, the snake determines whether the object is friend or (1) _____. If the object is a threat to the snake, the snake will bite the object with the intention of injecting its deadly (2) _____.

Word forms	"Give the verb form of these nouns and adjectives."
	1. perception → _____
	2. persuasive → _____
Word forms in cloze	"Fill in the blank with the correct form of the word in parentheses."
	(*perception*) 1. No one could _____ any difference between the two drinks.
	(*persuasive*) 2. Blackmail and flattery are two forms of _____.
Error identification	"One of the three underlined words is incorrect. Circle the error and write a correction above."
	1. <u>Due</u> to the heavy fog, the <u>fly</u> for Chicago was not able to take <u>off</u> on time.
	2. The jury found the defendant, who is a grandmother of twelve, <u>innocence</u> of the <u>heinous</u> crime, so the judge sentenced her to a <u>decade</u> in prison.
Answering questions (target vocabulary are in the question)	"Answer these questions."
	_____ 1. If you have a *dozen* doughnuts and then you give five to your friend, how many doughnuts do you have?
	_____ 2. If *venom* enters a young child's body, what will happen to the child?

Original sentences	"For each word, write an original sentence that shows that you know the meaning of the word." 1. *dozen* _____ _____ 2. *skinny* _____ _____
Original story	"Write a story about anything you want. Use 10 of these words in your story: *army, cattle, donkey, foe, ivory, lament, oath, portray, tortoise, venom.* Give your story a title." [*Note:* This can be a list of numbered sentences, a paragraph, or an essay—depending on what the students are accustomed to.] _____ _____ _____ _____

An important question for us to consider is, "What might make a given type of exercise more effective than another type of exercise?" Exercises can vary numerous ways, including amount of time required, degree of difficulty, number of vocabulary retrievals, and active or passive retrieval. Possible avenues for discussion include attention, depth of processing, number of retrievals, and spacing between retrievals.

The role of attention and noticing in second language acquisition has been an important and much debated topic (Schmidt, 1990, 1997; Truscott, 1998). In the strong form of Schmidt's Noticing

Hypothesis, noticing, or conscious awareness, is a necessary condition for learning. The orthodox position in psychology and cognitive science is that there is no learning without attention (Schmidt, 1995). In weaker versions, it is thought that noticing is helpful but perhaps not necessary for learning.

How could attention be a component in an exercise? A certain type of exercise might serve to make a particular L2 word more salient—i.e., it draws attention to the word. For example, in the common vocabulary exercise "odd-man out," learners have to find the one word that does not belong in the group: *steal, avalanche, thief, robbery*. Likewise, having to fill in a cloze exercise with target words should draw the learners' attention to those words.

In a study of second-semester L2 Spanish learners, Jourdenais, Ota, Stauffer, Boyson, and Doughty (1995) found that textual modification of learning material resulted in more noticing and in more use of the target language items. In this study, the researchers used an unenhanced and an enhanced version of a text. In the enhanced version, the target items were underlined and printed in a different font. Some target items were also put in bold font while others were shadowed. The fact that the target items looked different from the rest of the text caused them to be noticed. Since learners in this study tended to notice and pay more attention to forms that merely looked different in the text, then it can be assumed that an exercise that draws their attention to the target items would also have similar success.

The depth of processing model for learning was first proposed by Craik and Lockhart (1972) and later expanded upon by Craik and Tulving (1975). In this model, "the durability of memory traces is a direct consequence of encoding, with deeper and more elaborate encoding leading to more durable memory traces: the deeper the processing, the better the learning" (Schouten-van Parreren, 1995, p. 190). (For a convincing rationale challenging the validity of the depth of processing model at both a theoretical and practical level, see Hulstijn, 2001.)

Thus, in the case of vocabulary exercises, we might assume that writing an original sentence with a word requires deeper processing than answering a multiple choice question or matching the meaning of a word to the correct word. However, research has not addressed such practical application. While there is general consensus that deeper processing does result in better learning, it has remained unclear which factors specifically influence depth.

Schouten-van Parreren's (1995) review of the literature revealed three possible factors: elaboration, distinctiveness, and difficulty. Filling in a cloze exercise with target vocabulary words requires more *elaboration* by the learner than just looking at the list of target words. When a learner confuses one L2 word for another, it is often useful to make the word (artificially, sometimes) *distinct*. For example, a person learning the difference between deductive teaching and inductive teaching might remember that deductive, which begins with the letters *de-*, depends on the teacher (and depends begins with *de-*). On the other hand, inductive is independent of the teacher and both of these words begin with the letters *in-*. In more general terms, distinctiveness could also refer to a word with an unusual orthography or pronunciation, a characteristic that would make it more memorable. Finally, the degree of *difficulty* may influence depth of processing. Mondria and Wit-de Boer (1991) found that words whose meaning was relatively difficult to guess from a sentence context tended to be better recalled than words from simpler contexts.

Empirical studies comparing different types of exercises are indeed rare. Whether depth of processing or noticing or some other factor is the most important, no research has produced any results that allow us to categorize one exercise type as requiring more depth of knowledge than another. The following are three common example exercises for the word *selfish*:

(a) *A <u>selfish</u> person is: ___ good, ___ bad*

(b) *Write a sentence with <u>selfish</u>: _____*

(c) *Which of the following is something that a <u>selfish</u> person does? Choose two.*

    ___ *eat all of the candy instead of giving some to a friend*

    ___ *study all of the words for the examination tomorrow*

    ___ *insist on doing what he wants instead of what the group wants*

    ___ *buy a new car because it is very economical*

Even though it would seem that (a) requires less mental elaboration than (b) or (c), this has not been shown empirically. In the case of (b) versus (c), which one is "better"? While (c) is certainly longer and requires more L2 exposure, it is important to note that the exposure is not necessarily directed toward the meaning of *selfish*. The simple fact is that much more work needs to be done with practice exercises before we can say exactly which kinds of exercises require a greater degree of mental elaboration and rehearsal.

What has research shown regarding specific exercise types? One research study (Hulstijn, 1998) explored the question of whether writing words is more effective than just encountering words in a reading passage. The students were Dutch university EFL learners (n = 97). They were randomly assigned to one of three conditions. In condition 1, the students read a letter to the editor. Target words were in the letter. In condition 2, students read the letter and then did a gap-filling (i.e., fill in the blank) exercise. In condition 3, students were given the target words and told to write a letter to the editor. On a test given immediately after the experiment, the highest retention was in condition three, letter writing. Out of a perfect score of 10 (representing 10 words), condition 1 had an average of 4.3, condition 2 had an average of 5.9, and condition 3 had an average of 7.1.

Some people criticize these experiments as well as direct teaching of or direct interaction with vocabulary because they believe that retention is naturally high because the learners have just dealt with these words. To allay this fear, Hulstijn also conducted a "delayed" test some time later and found that condition 3 was still superior to the other conditions. From a perfect score of 10, condition 1 had an average retention of 2.6, condition 2 had an average of 4.0, and condition 3 had an average of 4.3.

These differences may not seem very great, but they are. They are great because the difference between any of these treatments was not the result of the teacher but rather the exercise. In other words, the "learning differential" that resulted is due to the material, the exercises. Students who do the exercises found in condition 3 will retain more vocabulary even before they sit down to commit vocabulary to memory in intentional learning. For these learners, their job will be easier since they will then face less unknown material.

Hulstijn (1998) also reported results on a "weather report" study with a similar research question. Students were assigned to one of two conditions. In condition one, students read a weather report on a computer. In condition two, students again used a computer to read a weather report but then had to write their own weather report. Students were able to use a bilingual dictionary on the computer to look up the meaning of any unknown word and obtain an L1 translation. Afterwards, the computer logs were analyzed to see which words had been looked up, and a test was created of those items. The mean for condition 1 was 3.8 (of 10); the mean for condition 2 was 4.6.

Laufer and Hulstijn (1998) reported on a similarly designed study conducted in both the Netherlands and Israel. The research question was whether "pushed output" using the target words resulted in better incidental vocabulary retention than comprehensible input containing the same target words.

The participants were from six groups of advanced EFL university learners, three groups in the Netherlands (87 learners) and three groups in Israel (99 learners). One group was randomly assigned to each of three experimental conditions. There was an immediate unannounced test and a delayed unannounced post-test.

In condition 1, students were provided with a text and a set of 10 multiple choice comprehension questions. The text was a 621-word letter to the editor of a British publication, *The Listener*, on a proposal of some members of parliament to amend the Obscene Publications Act. The target words were highlighted by putting them in bold print and glossed in L1 in the margin of the text. The task of the learners in this condition was to read the text and answer comprehension questions.

In condition 2, students were given the same text and the same questions. However, instead of appearing in bold print, the 10 target items were deleted from the passage and substituted with 10 blanks numbered 1 through 10. The 10 target items, along with given words that did not appear in the original text at all (i.e., they serve as distractors), were printed in random order as a list on a separate page. Both an L1 translation and an L2 explanation appeared by each of these 15 items. The task of the learners in this condition was to read the text, fill in the 10 blanks with the missing words from the list of 15 words, and answer the comprehension questions.

In condition 3, learners were not given the text. They were asked to write a composition in the form of a letter to the editor of a British newspaper regarding the proposal of some members of Parliament to amend the Obscene Publications Act. Learners were instructed to argue for or against censorship on video films. The final words of the instructions on the sheets given to students were as follows: "In your letter, YOU MUST USE THE FOLLOWING TEN WORDS. You may decide yourself in which order you will use them. Explanations of the words and examples of usage are given below." The same 10 words were given as in the reading condition. An example of this information for the target item *wrath* follows:

> WRATH *(noun, uncountable)*
> *Strong or fierce anger*
> Example: *The wrath of the opponents to the proposed bill was*
> *understandable.*
> *NL = gramschap (NL=Dutch; Hebrew translations were*
> *provided in Israel.)*

All of the tasks were administered during regular class time, and none of the tasks was presented as a vocabulary learning task. Time-on-task was different in the three conditions. Condition 1 took about 40 to 45 minutes, condition 2 took 50 to 55 minutes, and condition 3, 70 to 80 minutes. This is almost a two-fold difference. As can be seen in Table 12, condition 3 clearly produced the best vocabulary retention.

TABLE 12 Average Retention Scores on Immediate Test

Condition	1	2	3
Netherlands	2.7	2.9	4.9
Israel	1.8	3.9	6.9

The theory to explain these results is that exercises or activities that require more mental effort on the learners' part result in better retention. Thus, writing a letter using the 10 words requires more mental effort than completing a gap-filling exercise. Both of these require more mental effort than reading the passage did. In addition, Laufer and Hulstijn (1998) refer to "pushed output." Learners completing any activity or any exercise will have produced "output." However, in order for learning to take place, it may be necessary that learners go one step beyond this—i.e., that they stretch their current English ability to produce "pushed output." Learners need to go beyond producing what they already know or feel comfortable with.

If the type of exercise matters, it could also be due to the amount of attention focused on the target items or the depth of processing required by the exercise. It could be argued that writing a letter with all 10 target items focused the learners' attention on the words in a stronger way than did the other two activities. Another more plausible explanation is that in writing the letter, the learners had to keep track of all 10 meanings in their heads and constantly rearrange them to form a coherent letter. In other words, learners had to process the target words at a much deeper level and multiple times.

In this study, Laufer and Hulstijn found that the third exercise, original written production, resulted in more than twice as many acquired words than either of the other two exercises. Writing original language with the vocabulary could have had better vocabulary results because students were pushed to produce output instead of just receiving input (exercise 1) or simply filling in blanks (exercise 2). Another possible explanation for the higher retention is that in writing a letter (as opposed to writing separate, unconnected sentences), students are forced to plan how they will use each word. In reality, students often choose a word, write a sentence, and then erase that sentence because they want to use that word in another sentence. This building of the letter (or paragraph) *requires learners to interact with any single word multiple times.* Regardless of the explanation, exercise 3 did produce better results.

A drawback to practical use of this exercise is that it takes students much more time to do this activity than either of the other two. While writing an original letter, paragraph, or longer piece of prose may be a good learning exercise, it is usually impractical for teachers in many classroom settings. In Folse (1999), I compared three vocabulary practice exercises. In exercise 1, students wrote original, unconnected sentences with the target vocabulary. In exercise 2, students did one fill-in-the-blank exercise. In exercise 3, students completed three different fill-in-the-blank exercises—i.e., the one in exercise 2 plus two additional ones. The rationale for including this third exercise was that it took learners about three times to complete exercise 1 as it did exercise 2. Any difference between exercise 1 and exercise 2 could be due as easily to the exercise type as to time on task. To control for time on task, exercise 3 was introduced. Thus, time on task was similar for exercise 1 and exercise 3.

Results showed that students acquired more than twice as many words in exercise 3 as they did in either exercise 1 or 2. There was no statistically significant difference between the acquisition for exercises 1 and 2. Vocabulary retention in this study was tested in both a productive sentence-writing and passive word-recognition method. It is interesting to note that even though learners only completed fill-in-the-blank sentence items in exercise 3, the learners were able to produce a higher number of correct sentences with the words than students who had actually practiced writing original sentences with the words (exercise 1). Thus, a key factor to explain the success of exercise 3 here is multiple retrievals. As seen in the Laufer and Hulstijn (1998) study, what may be important is not what you do with the target word but rather how many times you do it. This study supports the notion that an extremely important factor in L2 vocabulary acquisition is the number of retrievals that a learner makes of a given word.

This is a very important finding. Many educators mistakenly label practice activities such as multiple choice or matching as "simple" or "shallow." Their thinking is that practice such as this does not lead to deeper learning or production the target vocabulary. There is no research to back this up. Who can say what goes on in the head of any individual learner as he or she interacts with a word in a practice activity? In fact, in Folse (1999), I found that even learners who only did "shallow practice" such as multiple choice questions were able to write original sentences as well as learners whose practice consisted of writing original sentences.

Another important finding from this study was that the writing of original sentences did not lead to better retention of new vocabulary by nonnative speakers than fill-in-the-blank completion items did. At the same time, this kind of activity would require a great deal more teacher time than the multiple choice exercises done by the other two groups of students.

What You Can Do . . .

1. Do something with vocabulary in EVERY lesson.

It does not matter whether you are teaching K–3, English in Japan, or a reading course, vocabulary is important. You should make a concerted effort to incorporate new vocabulary or review/recycle vocabulary in every lesson.

2. Once you teach vocabulary, you must *test* vocabulary.

What you test and how you test it tell students what you value. Students will respond to your expectations. If they know that you expect them to learn a certain amount of vocabulary in each week or in each unit of the book, they will do this. Therefore, it is imperative that you include vocabulary in your student assessment.

3. Vocabulary practices can take many forms; what appears to be most important is not the form of the exercise as much as the number of "forced retrievals" of the word or its meaning.

There are dozens of ways to practice vocabulary in textbook or classroom activities, such as matching, odd-man out, true-false, multiple choice, jeopardy games, writing sentences, gap filling, etc. A common fallacy is that the more elaborate an exercise looks, the more likely a learner is to retain a word that is practiced in that kind of activity. Research findings indicate that what is more important is not *what* you do with the word as much as *how often* you do this with the word.

Frequency of retrieval is key. After students have learned some vocabulary, the teacher should do a rapid-fire activity such as asking simple questions at various cognitive levels about the words. For example, if students have studied *avocado, gorilla, drought, vine, misty, humid, swing, vegetation, monkey,* and *python,* the teacher could ask these questions of the whole class to see who can answer first: (1) Which three words are related to plants? (2) Which word is a verb that means to move freely while hanging? (3) Which animal has cold blood? (4) What is the longest word? (5) There are some plants and some animals. Which is the only one that people usually eat? (6) Which word describes the opposite of humid? This kind of activity requires very little teacher preparation. It is important because it forces learners to retrieve the word or its meaning multiple times.

4. Make use of the vocabulary software as well as resources on the Internet.

There is much more practice material available on the Internet than in any textbook. The problem is finding the practice material that is suitable for your students' needs, age, proficiency level, and other demographic aspects. Evaluating computer-based L2 vocabulary materials is also complex because of the various options now available in learner software. In Folse and Chien (2003) we examine the efficacy of four types of annotations—namely text, audio, pictures, and video.

In addition to existing material, there are also many sites where you can type in a passage from your math book or history book and obtain a cloze passage or list of difficult vocabulary.

When choosing Internet activities or vocabulary software, choose "smart" materials that can remember words that your students have missed and then recycle those words more frequently. Again, frequency of retrieval is important. Items that have been missed should be retrieved shortly thereafter; words that have been retrieved correctly should have subsequently longer gaps between retrievals.

Conclusion

FROM THE VIEWPOINT of second language learners, learning vocabulary—learning the meaning of new words—is probably the most common activity in their whole experience of learning a new language. Unfortunately, it is also a very frustrating one. Until very recently, relatively little research had investigated the *teaching and learning* of second language vocabulary. Teachers, for example, received almost no real guidance from well-designed research studies on vocabulary. The larger field of second language acquisition was more interested in other areas such as grammar, contrastive analysis, comprehensible input, learner strategies, and motivation.

In the absence of informed guidance on vocabulary instruction, teachers dealt with vocabulary as they saw fit. Many (if not most) teachers simply ignored the importance of vocabulary; therefore, they were not teaching vocabulary. Some intentionally chose to ignore vocabulary teaching as they opted to teach learning strategies instead, while others emphasized grammar and sentence patterns over vocabulary. Still other teachers ignored vocabulary because they were not sure of exactly what to do with vocabulary in their classes. Over time, these and other personal beliefs were repeated, giving us the eight vocabulary myths that I have addressed in this book. All of these myths can be detrimental to our teaching effectiveness, and all of them can certainly hinder our students' second language vocabulary learning.

Myth 1 showed us how grammar has dominated second language

curricula from course objectives to textbooks. In spite of students' language problems with vocabulary and their expressed wishes for more vocabulary instruction, grammar is still given a much more important role in the curriculum than is vocabulary. ESL textbooks, including reading, writing, discussion, and even multiskill books, are designed around or at least take into account an overall grammar syllabus, but the same is not done for vocabulary.

Next, we dispelled the myth (2) that using lists of words to teach or learn vocabulary is in itself bad pedagogy. As with all things, too much of any one thing is by definition excessive. Recent trends in education have tainted anything connected with rote memorization, yet second language research does not show that memorizing lists of words is ineffective in learning. In fact, what is recommended for lower-proficiency students is a "vocabulary flood," something that would lend itself well to the learning of new vocabulary from lists.

The myth (3) that words should be presented and learned in semantic sets is clearly false. Almost all second language textbooks arrange vocabulary in semantic sets. We can easily find textbooks that teach words arranged in semantic sets such as family members, animal names, days of the week, and prepositions of movement. Findings from pertinent research explained why this all-too-common practice should be abandoned.

Myth 4 explored the use of word translations in second language vocabulary learning, one of the more controversial issues within all of vocabulary teaching and learning. Numerous research study findings have shown that learners retain words better when the words are initially learned with a first language translation than when they are accompanied by a picture, an L2 explanation, or an L2 example sentence. Here I am not advocating that the teacher translate in class. However, students who are writing a translation of a word should not be discouraged from doing so when their purpose is to make an individual note to help them remember the words later on when they study by themselves.

Without a doubt, learning to use context clues is one of the most valuable reading skills that learners can ever master—in their L1 or L2. However, when the goal is not reading help but rather vocabulary learning, research is clear: *use of context clues is not an efficient way to learn vocabulary.* In the discussion of Myth 5, we discussed the differences between L1 and L2 and how truths from L1 were being incorrectly applied to L2 learning. Teachers should continue to teach and value context clues, but this should never be a substitute for teaching vocabulary—and lots of it!

In the discussion of Myth 6, teachers had the opportunity to read about the latest work on vocabulary learning strategies. Teachers frequently ask me, "So what is the best way to learn lots of new vocabulary?" The answer is not the easy one that most teachers want. One of the most important findings from the recent studies was that good learners actually use several strategies, but the exact combination of these strategies varies from learner to learner. Each good learner has developed a set of strategies. Research has shown that the best vocabulary learners are those who have a plan of study and who apply this plan consistently. It really is the proverbial case of "slow but steady wins the race."

One of the most widely sold kinds of book in the world is the dictionary. For second language vocabulary learning, the myth (7) regarding this type of book is that learners should strive to use a monolingual (L1–L1) dictionary as soon as possible. Many teachers believe that a bilingual dictionary is in fact some kind of "crutch." For this reason, some teachers will not allow their students to even have a bilingual dictionary in class. However, research shows that using dictionaries results in better word retention and comprehension than not using one and that a bilingual dictionary entry is more likely to lead to word retention than a monolingual entry. There is no research to support the myth that a bilingual dictionary is a bad thing or that a monolingual dictionary is inherently better for ultimate word retention.

Finally, we saw that there is a myth (8) that vocabulary is being dealt with sufficiently in the curriculum. The truth is that vocabulary is lacking in the overall curriculum. In any class, the amount of vocabulary instruction depends on the individual teacher since vocabulary teaching is almost never systematically planned across the curriculum in any program. Furthermore, except for the few vocabulary textbooks that explicitly cover vocabulary, most ESL textbooks do not systemati-cally deal with vocabulary. Research has shown that instruction fol-lowed by vocabulary exercises leads to better retention than instruction followed by another activity, such as additional exposure to the words. In addition, research on practice activities has yielded very promising findings. Traditional exercises that teachers have thought important, such as having students write original sentences, do not aid in vocabu-lary retention as much as the easier-to-grade cloze exercises. Research has shown that what is important about a particular type of exercise is the number of times that the (design of the) exercise requires a learner to retrieve a word and its meaning. These findings have implications for teachers, curriculum writers, and materials writers.

In sum, we know so much more now than we did when vocabulary research exploded in second language research in the early 1990s. Armed with these research findings, classroom teachers now have spe-cific information and concrete activities to help teach vocabulary suc-cessfully to second language learners.

Works Cited

Ahmed, M.O. (1989). Vocabulary learning strategies. In P. Meara (Ed.) *Beyond words*. London: Centre for International Language Teaching and Research.

Alderson, J. (1984). Reading in a foreign language: A reading problem or a language problem? In J. Alderson & A. Urquhart (Eds.), *Reading in a foreign language* (pp. 1–27). London: Longman.

Al-Seghayer, K. (2001). The effect of multimedia annotation modes on L2 vocabulary acquisition: A comparative study. *Language Learning and Technology, 5*, 202–232.

Atkins, P., & Baddeley, A. (1998). Working memory and distributed vocabulary learning. *Applied Psycholinguistics, 19*(4), 537–552.

Atkinson, R. (1975). Mnemonics in second-language acquisition. *American Psychologist, 30*, 821–828.

Baddeley, A. (1990). *Human memory*. Hillsdale, NJ: Lawrence Erlbaum Associates.

Bahrick, H., Bahrick, L., Bahrick, A., & Bahrick P. (1993). Maintenance of foreign language vocabulary and the spacing effect. *Psychological Science, 4*, 316–321.

Beaton, A., Gruneberg, M., & Ellis, N. (1995). Retention of foreign vocabulary learned using the keyword method: A ten-year follow-up. *Second Language Research, 11*(2), 112–120.

Beck, I., McKeown, M., & Omanson, R. (1987). The effects and uses of diverse vocabulary instructional techniques. In M. McKeown & M. Curtis (Eds.), *The nature of vocabulary acquisition* (pp. 147–164). Hillsdale, NJ: Lawrence Erlbaum Associates.

Beck, I., Perfetti, C., & McKeown, M. (1982). Effects of text construction and instructional procedures for teaching word meanings on comprehension and recall. *Journal of Educational Psychology, 74,* 506–521.

Beech, P. (1997). *An investigation of the problems that young learners of English have using bilingual dictionaries.* Unpublished thesis, Aston University. Retrieved January 18, 2004, from http://222.tesolgreece.com/beech01.html

Bell, F., & LeBlanc, L. (2000). The language of glosses in L2 reading on computer: Learners' preferences. *Hispania, 83,* 274–285.

Bialystok, E. (1981). The role of conscious strategies in second language proficiency. *The Modern Language Journal, 65,* 24–35.

Bjork, R. (1988). Retrieval practice and the maintenance of knowledge. In M. Gruneberg, P. Morris, & R. Sykes (Eds.), *Practical aspects of memory: Current research and issues* (pp. 396–401). Chichester, UK: Wiley.

Brown, T., & Perry, F. (1991). A comparison of three learning strategies for ESL vocabulary acquisition. *TESOL Quarterly, 25*(4), 655–670.

Carter, R. (1987). Vocabulary and second/foreign language teaching. *Language Teaching, 20,* 3–16.

Carter, R., & McCarthy, M. (1988). *Vocabulary and language teaching.* London: Longman.

Chall, J. (1987). Two vocabularies for reading: Recognition and meaning. In M. McKeown & M. Curtis (Eds.), *The nature of vocabulary acquisition* (pp. 7–18). Hillsdale, NJ: Lawrence Erlbaum Associates.

Chun, D., & Plass, J. (1996). Effects of multimedia annotations on vocabulary acquisition. *The Modern Language Journal, 80*(2), 183–199.

Clipperton, R. (1994). Explicit vocabulary instruction in French immersion. *The Canadian Modern Language Review/La Revue Canadienne des Langues Vivantes, 50*(4), 736–749.

Coady, J., Magoto, J., Hubbard, P., Graney, J., & Mokhtari, K. (1993). High frequency vocabulary and reading proficiency in ESL readers. In T. Huckin, M. Haynes, & J. Coady (Eds.), *Second language reading and vocabulary learning* (pp. 217–228). Norwood, NJ: Ablex.

Cohen, A., & Aphek, E. (1981). Easifying second language learning. *Studies in Second Language Acquisition, 3*(2), 221–236.

Cooper, T. (1999). Processing of idioms by L2 learners of English. *TESOL Quarterly, 33*(2), 233–262.

Coxhead, A. (2000). A new academic word list. *TESOL Quarterly, 34*(2), 213–238.

Craik, F., & Lockhart, R. (1972). Levels of processing: A framework for memory research. *Journal of Verbal Learning and Verbal Behaviour, 11,* 671–684.

Craik, F., & Tulving, E. (1975). Depth of processing and the retention of words in episodic memory. *Journal of Experimental Psychology, 104*(3), 268–294.

Davis, F. (1944). Fundamental factors of comprehension in reading. *Psychometrika, 9*(3), 185–197.

de Groot, A., & Keijzer, R. (2000). What is hard to learn is easy to forget: The roles of word concreteness, cognate status, and word frequency in foreign language learning and forgetting. *Language Learning, 50*(1), 1–56.

Doughty, C., & Pica, T. (1986). "Information gap" tasks: Do they facilitate second language acquisition? *TESOL Quarterly, 20*(2), 305–325.

Duquette, L., Renie, D., & Laurier, M. (1998). The evaluation of vocabulary acquisition when learning French as a second language in a multimedia environment. *Computer Assisted Language Learning, 11,* 3–34.

Elley, W. (1989). Vocabulary acquisition from listening to stories. *Reading Research Quarterly, 24*(2), 174–187.

Ellis, R. (1994). Factors in the incidental acquisition of second language vocabulary from oral input: A review essay. *Applied Language Learning, 5*(1), 1–32.

Ellis, R., Tanaka, Y., & Yamazaki, A. (1994). Classroom interaction, comprehension and the acquisition of L2 word meanings. *Language Learning, 44*(3), 449–491.

Eskey, D. (1988). Holding in the bottom: An interactive approach to the language problems of second language readers. In P. Carrell, J. Deveine, & D. Eskey (Eds.), *Interactive approaches to second language reading.* Cambridge: Cambridge University Press.

Fan, M. (2003). Frequency of use, perceived usefulness, and the actual usefulness of second language vocabulary strategies: A study of Hong Kong learners. *The Modern Language Journal, 87*(2), 222–241.

Flaitz, J. (1998, May). *Exit survey of the English Language Institute at the University of South Florida.* Unpublished manuscript.

Folse, K. (1993). *Talk a lot: Communication activities for speaking fluency.* Ann Arbor: The University of Michigan Press.

Folse, K. (1996). *Discussion starters: Speaking fluency activities for advanced ESL/EFL students.* Ann Arbor: The University of Michigan Press.

Folse, K. (1997). *Beginning reading practices: Building reading and vocabulary strategies.* Ann Arbor: The University of Michigan Press.

Folse, K. (1999a). *Clear grammar 3: Activities for spoken and written communication.* Ann Arbor: The University of Michigan Press.

Folse, K. (1999b). *The effect of type of written practice activity on second language vocabulary retention.* Unpublished doctoral dissertation, University of South Florida, Tampa.

Folse, K. (2001). *A survey of ESL/EFL teacher preferences regarding student dictionary use.* Unpublished manuscript.

Folse, K. (2002). *One Japanese ESL learner's use of context clues to complete an assignment.* Unpublished manuscript.

Folse, K. (2003a). Applying second language research results in the design of more effective ESL discussion activites. *The CATESOL Journal, 15*(1), 1–12.

Folse, K. (2003b). *A study of the gap between ESL students' perceived knowledge and actual knowledge of vocabulary.* Unpublished manuscript.

Folse, K. (2004a). *A case study of vocabulary teaching in two classes in an intensive program at a U.S. university.* Unpublished manuscript.

Folse, K. (2004b). *An examination of what intensive ESL students perceive as important in the curriculum.* Unpublished manuscript.

Folse, K. (2004c). *Intermediate reading practices, 3rd ed.: Building reading and vocabulary skills.* Ann Arbor: The University of Michigan Press.

Folse, K., & Bologna, D. (2003). *Targeting listening and speaking: Strategies and activities for ESL/EFL students.* Ann Arbor: The University of Michigan Press.

Folse, K., & Chien, Y. (2003). Using L2 research on multimedia annotations to evaluate CALL vocabulary materials. *Sunshine State TESOL Journal, 2*(1), 25–37.

Gefen, R. (1987). Increasing vocabulary teaching in Israel schools. *English Teachers' Journal, 35,* 38–43.

Grace, C. (1998). Retention of word meanings inferred from context and sentence-level translations: Implications for the design of beginning-level CALL software. *The Modern Language Journal, 82*(4), 533–544.

Grace, C. (2000). Gender differences: Vocabulary retention and access to translation for beginning language learners in CALL. *The Modern Language Journal 84*, 214–224.

Graves, M. (1987). The roles of instruction in fostering vocabulary development. In M. McKeown & M. Curtis (Eds.), *The nature of vocabulary acquisition* (pp. 165–184). Hillsdale, NJ: Lawrence Erlbaum Associates.

Green, D., & Meara, P. (1995). Guest editorial. *Computer Assisted Language Learning, 8*(2–3), 97–101.

Gu, Y. (1994, March). *Vocabulary learning strategies of good and poor Chinese EFL learners.* Paper presented at annual meeting of the Teachers of English to Speakers of Other Languages (TESOL), Baltimore, MD.

Gu, Y. (2003). Vocabulary learning in a second language: Person, task, context and strategies. *TESL-EJ, 7*(2), 1–25.

Gu, Y., & Johnson, R. (1996). Vocabulary learning strategies and language learning outcomes. *Language Learning, 46*, 643–679.

Gu, Y., & Leung, C. (2002). Error patterns of vocabulary recognition for EFL learners in Beijing and Hong Kong. *Asian Journal of English Language Teaching, 12*, 121–141.

Haynes, M. (1993). Patterns and perils of guessing in second language reading. In T. Huckin, M. Haynes, & J. Coady (Eds.), *Second language reading and vocabulary acquisition* (pp. 46–64). Norwood, NJ: Ablex.

Haynes, M., & Baker, I. (1993). American and Chinese readers learning from lexical familiarization in English texts. In T. Huckin, M. Haynes, & J. Coady (Eds.), *Second language reading and vocabulary acquisition* (pp. 130–152). Norwood, NJ: Ablex.

Hazenberg, S., & Hulstijn, J. (1996). Defining a minimal receptive second-language vocabulary for non-native university students: An empirical investigation. *Applied linguistics, 17*(2), 145–163.

Hinkel, E. (2001). *Second language writers' text: Linguistic and rhetorical features.* Hillsdale, NJ: Lawrence Erlbaum Associates.

Hinkel, E., & Fotos, S. (2002). From theory to practice: A teacher's view. In E. Hinkel & S. Fotos (Eds.), *New perspectives on grammar teaching in second language classrooms* (pp. 1–12). Hillsdale, NJ: Lawrence Erlbaum Associates.

Huckin, T., & Bloch, J. (1993). Strategies for inferring word meaning in context: A cognitive model. In T. Huckin, M. Haynes, & J. Coady (Eds.), *Second language reading and vocabulary acquisition* (pp. 153–178). Norwood, NJ: Ablex.

Hulstijn, J. (1992). Retention of inferred and given word meanings: experiments in incidental vocabulary learning. In P. Arnaud, & H. Bejoint (Eds.), *Vocabulary and applied linguistics* (pp. 113–125). London: Macmillan Academic and Professional Limited.

Hulstijn, J. (1993). When do foreign-language readers look up the meaning of unfamiliar words? The influence of task and learner variables. *The Modern Language Journal, 77*(2), 139–147.

Hulstijn, J. (1998). *There is no learning without attention.* Paper presented at the annual meeting of the American Association of Applied Linguistics (AAAL), Seattle, WA.

Hulstijn, J. (2001). Intentional and incidental second-language vocabulary learning: A reappraisal of elaboration, rehearsal, and automaticity. In P. Robinson, (Ed.), *Cognition and second language instruction* (pp. 258–286). New York: Cambridge University Press.

Hulstijn, J., Hollander, M., & Greidanus, T. (1996). Incidental vocabulary learning by advanced foreign language students: The influence of marginal glosses, dictionary use, and reoccurrence of unknown words. *The Modern Language Journal, 80*(3), 327–339.

Hulstijn, J., & Laufer, B. (2001). Some empirical evidence for the involvement load hypothesis in vocabulary acquisition. *Language Learning, 51*(3), 539–558.

Hunt, A., & Beglar, D. (1998). Current research and practice in teaching vocabulary. *The Language Teacher, 22*, 7–11.

Jacobs, G., Dufon, P., & Hong, F. (1994). L1 and L2 glosses in reading passages: Their effectiveness for increasing comprehension and vocabulary knowledge. *Journal of Research in Reading, 17*(1), 19–28.

James, M. (1996). *Improving second language reading comprehension: A computer-assisted vocabulary development approach.* Unpublished doctoral dissertation, University of Hawaii, Manoa.

Joe, A. (1995). Task-based tasks and incidental vocabulary learning: A case study. *Second Language Research, 11*(2), 159–177.

Joe, A. (1998). What effects do text-based tasks promoting generation have on incidental vocabulary acquisition? *Applied Linguistics, 19*(3), 357–377.

Joe, A., Nation, P., & Newton, J. (1996). Vocabulary learning and speaking activities. *English Teaching Forum, 34*(1), 2–7.

Jones, F. (1995). Learning an alien lexicon: A teach-yourself case. *Second Language Research, 11*(2), 95–111.

Jourdenais, R., Ota, M., Stauffer, S., Boyson, B., & Doughty, C. (1995). Does textual enhancement promote noticing? A think-aloud protocol analysis. In R. Schmidt (Ed.), *Attention and awareness in foreign language learning* (pp. 1–63). Manoa: University of Hawaii Press.

Kameenui, E., Carnine, D., & Freschi, R. (1982). Effects of text construction and instructional procedures for teaching word meanings on comprehension and recall. *Reading Research Quarterly, 17*, 367–388.

Kameenui, E., Dixon, R., & Carnine, D. (1987). Issues in the design of vocabulary instruction. In M. McKeown, & M. Curtis (Eds.), *The nature of vocabulary acquisition* (pp. 129–146). Hillsdale, NJ: Lawrence Erlbaum Associates.

Kaspar, L. (1993). The keyword method and foreign language learning: A rationale for its use. *Foreign Language Annals, 26*(2), 244–251.

Kitajima, R. (2001). The effect of instructional conditions upon students' vocabulary retention: Output activities vs. input dominant activation. *Applied Language Learning, 12*, 55–80.

Knight, S. (1994). Dictionary use while reading: The effects on comprehension and vocabulary acquisition for students of different verbal abilities. *The Modern Language Journal, 78*(3), 285–299.

Koda, K. (1989). The effects of transferred vocabulary knowledge on the development of L2 reading proficiency. *Foreign Language Annals, 22*, 529–540.

Kojic-Sabo, I., & Lightbown, P. (1999). Students' approaches to vocabulary learning and their relationship success. *The Modern Language Journal, 83*(2), 176–192.

Krashen, S. (1982). *Principles and practice in second language acquisition.* New York: Prentice-Hall.

Krashen, S. (1989). We acquire vocabulary and spelling by reading: Additional evidence for the input hypothesis. *The Modern Language Journal 73*(4), 440–464.

Krashen, S. (1993). The case for free voluntary reading. *The Canadian Modern Language Review/La Revue Canadienne des Langues Vivantes, 50*(1), 72–82.

Kudo, Y. (1999). *L2 vocabulary learning strategies* (NFLRC NetWork #14). Honolulu: University of Hawaii, Second Language Teaching & Curriculum Center. Retrieved December 5, 2003, from http://www.nflrc.hawaii.edu/NetWorks/NW14/

Lawson, M., & Hogben, D. (1996). The vocabulary-learning strategies of foreign-language students. *Language Learning, 46*(1), 101–135.

Landauer, T., & Bjork, R. (1978). Optimum rehearsal patterns and name learning. In M. Gruneberg, P. Morris, & R. Sykes (Eds.), *Practical aspects of memory* (pp. 625–632). London: Academic Press.

Laufer, B. (1989). What percentage of lexis is essential for comprehension? In C. Lauren & M. Nordman (Eds.), *Special language: From humans thinking to thinking machines* (pp. 316–323). Clevedon, UK: Multilingual Matters.

Laufer, B. (1990). Why are some words more difficult than others? Some intralexical factors that affect the learning of words. *International Review of Applied Linguistics in Language Teaching, 28*(4), 293–307.

Laufer, B. (1992). How much lexis is necessary for reading comprehension? In P. Arnaud & H. Bejoint (Eds.), *Vocabulary and applied linguistics* (pp. 126–131). London: Macmillan Academic and Professional Limited.

Laufer, B. (1997). The lexical plight in second language reading: Words you don't know, words you think you know, and words you can't guess. In J. Coady & T. Huckin (Eds.), *Second language vocabulary acquisition* (pp. 20–34). Cambridge: Cambridge University Press.

Laufer, B. (1998a). The development of passive and active vocabulary in a second language: Same or different? *Applied Linguistics, 19*(2), 255–271.

Laufer, B. (1998b, March). *A case for pushed output in incidental vocabulary acquisition.* Paper presented at the annual meeting of American Association of Applied Linguistics (AAAL), Seattle, WA.

Laufer, B., & Hadar, L. (1997). Assessing the effectiveness of monolingual, bilingual, and "bilingualised" dictionaries in the comprehension and production of new words. *The Modern Language Journal, 81*(2), 189–196.

Laufer, B., & Hill, M. (2000). What lexical information L2 learners select in a CALL dictionary and how does it affect word retention? *Language Learning & Technology, 3*(2), 58–76.

Laufer, B., & Hulstijn, J. (1998, March). *What leads to better incidental vocabulary learning: Comprehensible input or comprehensible output?* Paper presented at the Pacific Second Language Research Form (PacSLRF), Tokyo.

Laufer, B., & Kimmel, M. (1997). Bilingualised dictionaries: How learners really use them. *System, 25*(3), 361–369.

Laufer, B., & Nation, P. (1995). Vocabulary size and use: Lexical richness in L2 written production. *Applied Linguistics, 16*(3), 307–322.

Laufer, B., & Paribakht, T. (1998). The relationship between passive and active vocabularies: Effects of language learning context. *Language Learning, 48*, 365–391.

Laufer, B., & Shmueli, K. (1997). Memorizing new words: Does teaching have anything to do with it? *RELC Journal, 28*(1), 89–108.

Laufer, B., & Sim, D. (1985). Measuring and explaining the reading threshold needed for English for academic purposes texts. *Foreign Language Annals, 18*, 405–411.

Laufer, B., & Yano, Y. (2001). Understanding unfamiliar words in a text: Do L2 learners understand how much they don't understand? *Reading in a Foreign Language, 13*(2), 549–566.

Leeke, P., & Shaw, P. (2000). Learners' independent records of vocabulary *System, 28*, 271–289.

Lessard-Clouston, M. (1994). Challenging student approaches to ESL vocabulary development. *TESL Canada Journal/Revue TESL du Canada, 12*(1), 69–80.

Lessard-Clouston, M. (1996, August). *Vocabulary acquisition in an academic discipline: ESL learners and theology.* Paper presented at the 11th World Congress of Applied Linguistics (AILA '96), University of Jyvaskyla, Finland.

Lewis, M. (1993). *The lexical approach*. Hove, UK: Language Teaching Publications.

Lewis, M. (1997). *Implementing the lexical approach*. Hove, UK: Language Teaching Publications.

Liu, D. (2003). The most frequently used spoken American English idioms: A corpus analysis and its implications. *TESOL Quarterly, 37*(4), 671–700.

Lomicka, L. (1998). "To gloss or not to gloss": An investigation of reading comprehension online. *Language Learning and Technology, 1*(2): 41–50.

Long, M. (1989). *Task, group, and task-group interactions*. Paper delivered at RELC Seminar, Singapore.

Long, M., & Porter, P. (1985). Group work, interlanguage talk, and second language acquisition. *TESOL Quarterly, 19*, 207–228.

Lotto, L., & de Groot, A. (1998). Effects of learning method and word type on acquiring vocabulary in an unfamiliar language. *Language Learning, 48*(1), 31–69.

Ludwig, J. (1984). Vocabulary acquisition as a function of word characteristics. *The Canadian Modern Language Review/La Revue Candienne des Langues Vivantes, 40*(5), 552–562.

Luppescu, S., & Day, R. (1993). Reading, dictionaries, and vocabulary learning. *Language Learning, 43*(2), 263–287.

McCarthy, M. (1994). A new look at vocabulary in EFL. *Applied Linguistics, 5*(1), 12–22.

McKeown, M., Beck, I., Omanson, R., & Pope, M. (1985). Some effects of the nature and frequency of vocabulary instruction on the knowledge and use of words. *Reading Research Quarterly, 20*(5), 522–535.

McKeown, M., & Curtis, M. (Eds.), (1987). *The nature of vocabulary acquisition*. Hillsdale, NJ: Lawrence Erlbaum Associates.

Mackey, W. (1965). *Language teaching analysis*. London: Longman.

Maiguashca, R. (1984). Semantic fields: Towards a methodology for teaching vocabulary in the second-language classroom. *The Canadian Modern Language Review/La Revue Canadienne des Langues Vivantes, 50*(1), 274–297.

Maiguashca, R. (1993). Teaching and learning vocabulary in a second language: Past, present, and future directions. *The Canadian Modern*

Language Review/La Revue Canadienne des Langues Vivantes, 50(1), 83–100.

Margosein, C., Pascarella, E., & Pfaum, S. (1982). The effects of instruction using semantic mapping on vocabulary and comprehension. *Journal of Early Adolescence,* (2), 185–194.

Martin, M. (1984). Advanced vocabulary teaching: The problem of synonyms. *The Modern Language Journal, 68*(2), 130–137.

Meara, P. (1980). Vocabulary acquisition: A neglected aspect of language learning. *Language Teaching and Linguistics Abstracts, 13,* 221–246.

Miller, G. (1956). The magical number seven, plus or minus two: Some limits on our capacity for processing information. *The Psychological Review, 63,* 81–97.

Mondria, J., & Wit-de Boer, M. (1991). The effects of contextual richness on the guessability and the retention of words in a foreign language. *Applied Linguistics, 12,* 249–267.

Morrison, L. (1996). Talking about words: A study of French as a second language learners' lexical inferencing procedures. *The Canadian Modern Language Review, 53*(1), 41–75.

Nagata, N. (1999). The effectiveness of computer assisted interactive glosses. *Foreign Language Annals, 32–34,* 469–479.

Nagy, W., & Herman, P. (1987). Breadth and depth of vocabulary knowledge: Implications for acquisition and instruction. In M. McKeown & M. Curtis (Eds.), *The nature of vocabulary acquisition* (pp. 19–36). Hillsdale, NJ: Lawrence Erlbaum Associates.

Nassaji, H. (2003). L2 vocabulary learning from context: Strategies, knowledge sources, and their relationship with success in L2 lexical inferencing. *TESOL Quarterly, 37*(4), 645–670.

Nation, I.S.P. (1982). Beginning to learn foriegn vocabulary: A review of the research. *RELC Journal, 13*(1), 14–36.

Nation, P. (1993). Measuring readiness for simplified material: A test of the first 1,000 words of English. In M. Tickoo (Ed.), *Simplification: Theory and application* (pp. 193–202). Singapore: RELC.

Nation, P. (Ed.). (1994). *New ways in teaching vocabulary.* Alexandria, VA: Teachers of English to Speakers of Other Languages.

Nation, P. (2000). Learning vocabulary in lexical sets: Dangers and guidelines. *TESOL Journal, 9*(2), 6–10.

Nation, P. (2001). *Learning vocabulary in another language.* New York: Cambridge University Press.

Nation, P., & Coady, J. (1988). Vocabulary and reading. In R. Carter & M. McCarthy (Eds.), *Vocabulary learning and teaching* (pp. 97–110). London: Longman.

Nattinger, J. (1988). Some current trends in vocabulary teaching. In R. Carter & M. McCarthy (Eds.), *Vocabulary learning and teaching* (pp. 62–81). London: Longman.

Nattinger, J., & DeCarrico, J. (1992). *Lexical phrases and language teaching.* Oxford: Oxford University Press.

Newton, J. (1991). *Negotiation: Negotiating what?* Paper given at SEAMEO Conference of Language Acquisition and the Second/Foreign Language Classroom, Singapore.

Newton, J. (1995). Task-based interaction and incidental vocabulary learning: A case study. *Second Language Research, 11*(2), 159–177.

Olsen, S. (1999). Errors and compensatory strategies: A study of grammar and vocabulary in texts written by Norwegian learners of English. *System, 27*(2), 191–206.

O'Malley, J., & Chamot, A. (1993). *Learning strategies in second language acquisition.* Cambridge: Cambridge University Press.

O'Malley, J., Chamot, A., Stewner-Manzanares, G., Kupper, L., & Russo, R. (1985). Learning strategies used by beginning and intermediate ESL students. *Language Learning, 35,* 21–46.

Ott, C., Butler, D., Blake, R., & Ball, J. (1973). The effect of interactive-image elaboration on the acquisition of foreign language vocabulary. *Language Learning, 23*(2), 197–206.

Oxford, R. (1990). *Language learning strategies: What every teacher should know.* Boston: Heinle & Heinle.

Oxford, R. (1992/93). Language learning strategies in a nutshell: Update and ESL suggestions. *TESOL Journal, 2*(2), 18–22.

Padilla, A., & Sung, H. (1990). Information processing and foreign language learning. In A. Padilla, H. Fairchild, & C. Valadez (Eds.),

Foreign language education: Issues and strategies (pp. 41–55). Newbury Park, CA: Sage Publications.

Paribakht, T., & Wesche, M. (1993). Reading comprehension and second language development in a comprehension-based ESL program. *TESL Canada Journal, 11*(1), 9–29.

Paribakht, T., & Wesche, M. (1996). Enhancing vocabulary acquisition through reading: A hierarchy of text-related exercise types. *The Canadian Modern Language Review/La Revue Canadienne des Langues Vivantes, 52*(2), 155–178.

Paribakht, T., & Wesche, M. (1997). Vocabulary enhancement activities and reading for meaning in second language vocabulary acquisition. In J. Coady & T. Huckin (Eds.), *Second language vocabulary acquisition,* (pp. 174–200). Cambridge: Cambridge University Press.

Paribakht, T., & Wesche, M. (1999). Reading and "incidental" L2 vocabulary acquisition. *Studies in Second Language Acquisition, 21,* 195–224.

Parry, K. (1993). Too many words: Learning the vocabulary of an academic subject. In T. Huckin, M. Haynes, & J. Coady (Eds.), *Second language reading and vocabulary learning* (pp. 46–64). Norwood, NJ: Ablex.

Pica, T., & Doughty, C. (1985a). Input and interaction in the communicative language classroom: A comparison of teacher fronted and group activities. In S. Gass & C. Madden (Eds.), *Input in second language acquisition* (pp. 115–132). Rowley, MA: Newbury House.

Pica, T., & Doughty, C. (1985b). The role of group work in classroom second language acquisition. *Studies in Second Language Acquisition, 7,* 233–248.

Pimsleur, P. (1967). A memory schedule. *The Modern Language Journal, 51*(2), 73–75.

Pino-Silva, J. (1993). Untutored vocabulary acquisition and L2 reading ability. *Reading in a Foreign Language, 9*(2), 845–857.

Politzer, R., & McGroarty, M. (1985). An exploratory study of learning behaviors and their relationship to gains in linguistic and communicative competence. *TESOL Quarterly, 19*(1), 103–123.

Pressley, M., & Ahmad, M. (1986). Transfer of imager-based mnemonics by adult learners. *Contemporary Educational Psychology, 11,* 150–160.

Pressley, M., Levin, J., Kuiper, N., Bryant, S., & Michener, S. (1982). Mnemonic versus non-mnemonic vocabulary-learning strategies: Additional comparisons. *Journal of Educational Psychology, 74*(5), 693–707.

Pressley, M., Levin J., & McDaniel, M. (1987). Remembering versus inferring what a word means: Mnemonic and contextual approaches. In M. McKeown & M. Curtis (Eds.), *The nature of vocabulary acquisition* (pp. 107–128). Hillsdale, NJ: Lawrence Erlbaum Associates.

Prince, P. (1995). Second language vocabulary learning: The role of context versus translations as a function of proficiency. *The Modern Language Journal, 80*(4), 478–493.

Rasekh, Z., & Ranjbary, R. (2003). Metacognitive strategy training for vocabulary learning. *TESL-EJ, 7*(2), 1–15.

Richards, J. (1976). The role of vocabulary teaching. *TESOL Quarterly, 10*(1), 77–89.

Rivers, W., & Temperley, M. (1978). *A practical guide to the teaching of English as a second or foreign language.* New York: Oxford University Press.

Roby, W. (1999). What's in a gloss? *Language Learning and Technology, 2*(2), 94–101.

Rubin, J. (1975). What the "good language learner" can teach us. *TESOL Quarterly, 9*(1), 41–51.

Sanaoui, R. (1995). Adult learners' approaches to learning vocabulary in second languages. *The Modern Language Journal, 79*(1), 15–28.

Sanaoui, R. (1996). Processes of vocabulary instruction in ten French as a second language classrooms. *The Canadian Modern Language Review, 53*(2), 179–199.

Schatz, E., & Baldwin, R. (1986). Context clues are unreliable predictors of word meanings. *Reading Research Quarterly, 21*(4), 439–453.

Schmidt, R. (1990). The role of consciousness in second language learning. *Applied Linguistics, 11*, 129–158.

Schmidt, R. (1995). Consciousness and foreign language learning: A tutorial on the role of attention and awareness in learning. In R. Schmidt (Ed.), *Attention and awareness in foreign language learning* (pp. 1–63). Manoa: University of Hawaii Press.

Schmidt, R. (1997, October). *There is no learning without attention.* Paper presented at the annual meeting of the Second Language Research Forum (SLRF), Lansing, MI.

Schmitt, N. (1998a). Measuring collocational knowledge: Key issues and an experimental assessment procedure. *ITL, 119–120,* 27–47.

Schmitt, N. (1998b). Quantifying word association responses: What is native-like? *System, 26,* 389–401.

Schmitt, N. (1998c). Tracking the incremental acquisition of second language vocabulary: A longitudinal study. *Language Learning, 48*(2), 281–317.

Schmitt, N., & Schmitt, D. (1993). Identifying and assessing vocabulary learning strategies. *Thai TESOL Bulletin, 5*(4), 27–33.

Schmitt, N., & Schmitt, D. (1995). Vocabulary notebooks: Theoretical underpinnings and practical suggestions. *ELT Journal, 49,* 133–143.

Schmitt, N., & Zimmerman, C. (2002). Derivative word forms: What do learners know? *TESOL Quarterly, 36*(2), 145–171.

Schouten-van Parreren, C. (1995). Action psychology as applied to foreign language vocabulary acquisition. *Computer Assisted Language Learning, 8*(2–3), 181–204.

Sciarone, A., & Meijer, P. (1995). Does practice make perfect? On the effect of exercises on second/foreign language acquisition. *ITL, 107–108,* 35–57.

Snellings, P., van Gelderen, A., & de Glopper, K. (2002). Lexical retrieval: An aspect of fluent second-language production that can be enhanced. *Language Learning, 52*(4), 723–754.

Stahl, S., & Clark, C. (1987). The effects of participatory expectations in classroom discussion on the learning of science vocabulary. *American Educational Research Journal, 24*(4), 541–545.

Stanovich, K. (1986). Matthew effect in reading: Some consequences of individual differences in the acquisition of literacy. *Reading Research Quarterly, 21,* 360–407.

Sternberg, R. (1987). Most vocabulary is learned from context. In M. McKeown & M. Curtis (Eds.), *The nature of vocabulary acquisition* (pp. 89–106). Hillsdale, NJ: Lawrence Erlbaum Associates.

Tall, G., & Hurman, J. (2000). Using a dictionary in a written French examination: The students' experience. *Language Learning Journal, 21*, 50–56.

Tinkham, T. (1993). The effects of semantic clustering on the learning of second language vocabulary. *System, 21* (3), 371–380.

Tinkham, T. (1997). The effects of semantic and thematic clustering on the learning of second language vocabulary. *Second Language Research, 13*(2), 138–163.

Tréville, M. (1996). Lexical learning and reading in L2 at the beginner level: The advantage of cognates. *Canadian Modern Language Review, 53*(1), 173–190.

Truscott, J. (1998). Noticing in second language acquisition: A critical review. *Second Language Research, 14*, 103–135.

Waring, R. (1997). The negative effects of learning words in semantic sets. *System, 25*(2), 261–274.

Watanabe, Y. (1997). Input, intake, and retention: Effects of increased processing on incidental learning of foreign language vocabulary. *Studies in Second Language Acquisition, 19*, 287–307.

Wenden, A. (1986). What do second language learners know about their language learning? A second look at retrospective accounts. *Applied Linguistics, 7*(2), 186–201.

Wenden, A., & Rubin, J. (Eds.). (1987). *Learner strategies in language learning*. Englewood Cliffs, NJ: Prentice-Hall International.

Wesche, M., & Paribakht, T. (1994, March). *Enhancing vocabulary acquisition through reading: A hierarchy of text-related exercise types*. Paper presented at the meeting of the American Association for Applied Linguistics (AAAL), Baltimore, MD.

West, M. (1953). *A general service list of English words*. Longman, London.

Wilkins, D. (1972). *Linguistics in language teaching*. London: Arnold.

Xue, G., & Nation, I.S.P. (1984). A University Word List. *Language Learning and Communication, 3*(2), 215–229.

Yavuz, H. (1963). The retention of incidentally learned connotative responses. *Journal of Psychology, 55*, 409–418.

Yavuz, H., & Bousfield, W. (1959). Recall of connotative meaning. *Psychological Reports, 5*, 319–320.

Yu, L. (1996). The role of the L1 in the acquisition of motion verbs in English by Chinese and Japanese learners. *Canadian Modern Language Review, 53*(1), 191–218.

Zahar, R., Cobb, T., & Spada, N. (2001). Acquiring vocabulary through reading: Effects of frequency and contextual richness. *Canadian Modern Language Review, 57*(4), 541–572.

Zimmerman, C. (1997). Do reading and interactive vocabulary instruction make a difference? An empirical study. *TESOL Quarterly, 31*(1), 121–140.

Index